a single journey

BIBLICAL SKETCHES
FOR LIFE ON YOUR OWN

James McNutt

VINE
BOOKS

SERVANT PUBLICATIONS
ANN ARBOR, MICHIGAN

Vine Books is an imprint of Servant Publications especially designed to serve evangelical Christians.

Published by Servant Publications
P.O. Box 8617
Ann Arbor, Michigan 48107

Cover illustration: Pont Japonais, Bassin Aux Nympheas, by Claude Monet Christie's Images/Superstock Fine Art. Used by permission.

00 01 02 10 9 8 7 6 5 4 3 2

Printed in the United States of America
ISBN 1-56955-053-0

LIBRARY OF CONGRESS CATALOGING-IN-PUBLICATION DATA

McNutt, James, 1926-
    A single journey / James McNutt.
        p.   cm.
    ISBN 1-56955-053-0 (alk. paper)
    1. Single people—Religious life.   2. Single people in the Bible.   I. Title.
    BV4596.S5M37   1999
    248.8'4—dc21   98-49327
                                                        CIP

to julie,
the one single who just wouldn't leave me alone

contents

Acknowledgments 7

Introduction 9

1. The Ache That Wouldn't Go Away
   Adam: The World's Loneliest Single 15

2. You Can't Play on My Team, Kid
   Hagar: A Rejected Single Parent Who Discovered God's Care . . 35

3. All Stressed Up and No Place to Grow?
   Joseph: The Single Who Knew What to Do With Stress 59

4. Love Jericho Style
   Rahab: The Single Who Gave Up on Promiscuity 73

5. What If God Came to Your Pity Party?
   Elijah: The Single Who Was Depressed 91

6. How Can We Feel Close When You're So Near?
   Samson: The Hunk Who Couldn't Find Intimacy 111

7. The Way to a Man's Heart Is *Not* Through His Left Ventricle
   Ruth: The Widow Who Found the Recipe for Remarriage 129

8. Caring Enough to Care
   Jonah: The Single Who Couldn't Feel Compassion 149

9. Hanging Super Tough When the Going Gets Rough
   Daniel: The Single Who Had the Courage of His Convictions . . 167

10. So You Thought Felix and Oscar Were the Original
    Odd Couple?
    Mary and Martha: Two Singles Who Valued Friendship 191

11. Winning at Work Without Losing With God
Lydia: A Working Woman Who Almost Had It All. *209*

12. Finding Purpose for Every Single Day
Paul: A Man Who Made the Most of His Singleness *227*

13. Single Summa Cum Laude
Jesus: The Ultimate Single *245*

acknowledgments

My special appreciation to Pastor Jim Welch, a caring man of vision, who was brave enough to push in the clutch and shift our singles' ministry into first gear. Also my special admiration for Bob and Mary Kuhlman, who helped keep us headed in the right direction as we picked up speed.

And my very special thanks for the singular love, inspiration, and patience over the years of Glen, Edith, Gene, Rosemary, Joyce, Mary, Nancy, DoraLou, Jerry, Janet, Pat, Verlee, Millie, Marilyn, Beverly, Neva, Bertha, Mary Ann, Dolly, Donna, and Joanie. They weren't just along for the ride.

I express my gratitude not only to these long-time passengers, but also to the hundreds of others they represent who were kind enough to travel with us until we reached our respective stations and had to say good-bye.

introduction

O ne day in 1969 a middle-aged man I didn't know came up to me after church and said, "Hi, my name's Frank. Our Sunday school class is getting tired of hearing my voice. How would you like to teach the singles?"

I remember my immediate response: "What's a single?"

Frank answered with a brief, rather superficial explanation of what a single adult was.

"I'll do it," I said, perhaps a little too quickly.

Frank didn't know that I was desperate to get a Sunday school class. And I didn't know that I was about to begin a love affair with singles that continues to this day.

The term *single* was new and not popular back in that decade when our nation was being rocked by radical social change. There was something slightly disrespectful about the term. Sleazy tabloids were pitched to "singles." Some people had the idea that "single" meant "swinger," and sometimes it did. So not everyone who had never married or who had survived a divorce was ready to run out into the street yelling, "I'm a single. I'm a single!"

If I didn't know what a single was when I accepted Frank's class, I did know that a good teacher must understand his students in order to make his material relevant. So I bought and read every book on singles I could find. That didn't take much cash or time, for there was hardly anything on the market, especially for Christians. Church leaders were still scratching their heads trying to decide what to do with these unmarried "misfits," especially those who were casualties from the rising divorce rate.

Divorce was a problem then, because everyone was a little embarrassed when homes broke up in the church. Christians were supposed to have it all together, especially when it came to marriage. Some pastors, embarrassed by what they considered personal failure, decided to ignore the problem and hoped it would go away. Others, seeing their pastoral role as one of offering special care to the wounded and hurting, pioneered unique ministries tailored to the special needs of singles.

Singles loved it. At last they could meet with others who shared common experiences. "I thought I was the only one!" we frequently heard from newcomers. Unlike in the rest of the church, with its family-focused ministry, here were people who understood, who cared.

Sometimes it was a risky business. The discrimination singles felt was occasionally directed toward their leaders. My wife and I had friends who stopped speaking to us because they thought our work with singles meant we approved of divorce. A more difficult problem was the social misfits a singles' group attracted, who caused problems and were usually beyond our ability to help.

Today there are flourishing singles' ministries in churches all over America and the world. Divorce still packs the same destructive force that sends its radiating shock waves through hearts and hits even family and friends. Only now has the church come to accept it as an unfortunate but real part of the culture in which we live. And as young people wait longer to marry, the church is not so apt to say, "You're not married? What's wrong with you?" We've begun to accept the realities of our fragmented society and minister to the needs we face in and among us.

One thing doesn't change and that's human need. I wrote this book for singles because I believe their needs have not changed since I first started trying to find out what they were. I tried to incorporate the things they've taught me both in this country and in Brazil, where my wife, Julie, and I served as missionaries.

Our classroom was sometimes the family room floor, the front room couch, a desert campground, a mountain cabin, and often a kitchen. We laughed a lot, and sometimes we cried, but through it all we moved forward together in our walk with Christ. I hope these pages will encourage you to keep that walk going for as long as you continue your journey as a single adult.

Together we'll look at the lives of thirteen singles in the Bible. Starting with Adam, the first single, we'll identify a major problem in each life and show how each person worked together with God to solve it. Adam may have been the first single to deal with loneliness, but he will certainly not be the last. Next we'll walk with Hagar, who experienced a special touch from God after the rejection of people close to her almost ended her life. Joseph (that paragon of righteousness), we may be surprised to find, was a kind of human yo-yo. He

was up and then down, as stressful and unpredictable circumstances swirled around him. He didn't have access to a modern medicine chest or a psychiatrist. How did he handle it?

What more shall I say? Do we have time to see how by
faith Rahab escaped a promiscuous lifestyle, how God helped
Elijah through severe depression, how Ruth prepared for a
second marriage? Jonah flunked Compassion 101, but we
needn't. Daniel models conviction under pressure; Mary and
Martha are unlikely roomies who manage to be friends; Lydia
shows us how a working woman keeps her balance; Paul is
the remarkable single with a single focus. Finally, we'll view
Jesus, the second and last Adam, as the ultimate single.

Now, after reading this list of names, I know the question
you're about to ask. Let me answer it before you get me into
trouble. There is no way we can know for dead, absolute sure
that every single one of these Bible personalities was single.
Most, assuredly, were. For a few others, all we can do is apply
the well-known Duck Principle: If the person talks like a
single (never mentions a spouse) and walks like a single
(encounters problems that may be just a bit more characteristic of the single life), then that person must be a single.

There are several ways you can use this book. The thirteen
chapters are intended to be something more than just a pleasant exploration of Bible personalities. My hope is that you'll
also want to read the biblical narrative and then answer the
questions at the end of each chapter. Going the "second
mile" may be what's required for God to bring about the
changes in your life that he desires. In addition, each study
was designed, and yea verily actually tested, at meetings and
as Sunday school curriculum for singles. Readers with the gift

of teaching may want to go and do likewise.

Now, a final word. As it is my desire to protect both the innocent and the not-so-innocent, the people, places, and actual circumstances in the anecdotes I've used in this book have been fictionalized or presented as composites.

the ache that wouldn't go away

Adam: The World's Loneliest Single

For Adam's story, see Genesis 2.

On that primeval afternoon, as the sun moved into the western sky, God went looking for Adam, to initiate a chat. God found him in a grassy glade, romping with some new animal acquaintances. Seeing how Adam and God were the best of friends, I imagine their conversation went something like this:

"I've about finished some very creative and exciting work. It all looks very good, and I'm taking the day off."

"Sounds like a winner, Lord!"

"I'd like you to get in the habit too, Adam. So why don't you take the day off? We can relax and talk."

"Sounds even better, Lord."

"I know you haven't had much time to look around, but how do you like our planet so far?"

"Well, Lord, I hope you won't think I'm a complainer, but. ..."

"Is something wrong, Adam?"

"I shouldn't have said anything."

"Don't you find the garden pleasant?"

"It's wonderful. You might even say Edenic."

"How's the food?"

"I'm stuffed. Nobody goes hungry in this place."

"Your work, perhaps?"

"Horticulture's fine, Lord. Looks like I'll be finding new specimens forever."

"Perhaps. But I know just cultivating the plants won't satisfy a fine mind like yours for very long. How are you getting along with that menagerie I made?"

"No problem. You've got some sense of humor!"

"I hoped you'd notice. Tomorrow we'll have a few more laughs together. I want you to name those creatures, any and all of them."

"Bright and early! Now about my problem ..."

"We'll talk about that later, Adam."

"Whatever you say, Lord. I'll be ready first thing for the animals. But say, Lord ..."

"Yes, Adam?"

"There are so many. Do you think you could get them organized and have them march by single file?"

A Dream and Heart's Desire

Every new day is full of incredible surprises, Adam mused, as he bedded down. He snuggled under his leafy covering and conjured up names. Soon wakefulness gave way to the most wonderful dream. He had apparently named all the animals. Then one last creature closely resembling his own appearance emerged from the forest, gave him a beguiling smile, and purposefully strode toward him.

Adam stood and smiled back. "I am man," he said, "and you are—"

Adam awoke with a start. Light was already showing in the east. He raced for the rocky outcropping he had chosen as a reviewing stand for the world's first parade. And what a parade it promised to be! Everything that flew, walked, slithered, or hopped was about to break into the clearing and march past the first and prototypical man.

Aardvark, addax, adder …

Adam was flexing his lexicographic muscles when the first two creatures ambled by. Adam noticed they weren't coming single file as he had requested. "Aardvark, male and female," he announced. Turning to his left he saw two magnificent beasts approaching. "Look at those horns! I'll call those addaxes. Over there, we have a pair of … adders. And here come two …" A voice interrupted and Adam looked up.

"Adam, you're very clever, but you don't have to do this in alphabetical order."

Finally the parade ended. Exhausted, Adam stepped down from his perch and lay back on the cool grass of the clearing. In his head was an enormous list of new words that ranged from aardvark to zebu. The completion of this monumental task was in itself exhilarating, but somehow the gnawing, bewildering emptiness he felt had greatly intensified.

He remembered the dream—the beguiling smile!

A clump of leaves fluttered at the edge of the clearing. Adam jumped to his feet. Perhaps the "other" he yearned for was about to emerge. Adam turned slowly away. It was only a puff of wind rustling the branches.

Moments later, with a cry of utter desolation, Adam fell to

the grass, his body wracked with sobs that welled up from his innermost being. Adam knew that he alone among God's creatures was without a companion.

Alone Again, or Still

Like their prototypical forebear, Adam, contemporary singles grapple with the age-old dilemma of loneliness. Whether they're sipping wine in a dimly lit singles' bar or clutching Styrofoam cups of lukewarm coffee at a singles' gathering in the church basement, the same nagging questions surface again and again:

"Why am I so lonely?"

"What *is* loneliness?"

"How can I escape the loneliness I experience every single day?"

To answer these questions, perhaps we need to remind ourselves of something Adam soon discovered: being solitary was never God's purpose for mankind. Genesis 2:18 says: "It is not good for the man to be 'in his singleness,'" as the original Hebrew puts it. The negative *not* is in the strongest form possible. It's as if God were saying, "Adam, it's not good, not good at all, for you to be alone."

With this emphatic announcement so early in God's relationship with man, should we be surprised that it becomes a major motif in the biblical symphony of truth? Community, togetherness, oneness, unity, friendship, fellowship, brotherhood—all are intriguing facets of the progressive development of life in relationship with others.

Today's single hardly needs a divine revelation to sense that there is something better than being alone. But if being alone isn't God's will, why are you or others you know alone and lonely? In Adam's unique situation, there was simply no one out there. Singles today face a different problem: the distinct possibility of being lonely, even in the company of quite a crowd of Adam's progeny.

Unfortunately, some people try to run from loneliness through an exit door that is mismarked. Whoever posted the signs was deceived or intentionally set out to deceive others.

Every singles' group, unfortunately, seems to have a member like a man we'll call Ralph, usually a divorcé. His "exit loneliness" sign is on the outside of any bedroom door. His modus operandi is dinner, followed by dessert, which, as he charmingly explains, his date should be happy to provide. Because Ralph never learned to experience real intimacy, he deceives himself year after year with the pseudointimacy of many contacts, but no relationships.

Another counterfeit solution is activity. A multimillion-dollar industry has grown out of this deception. It's as if singles are told they will get well from motion. So keep moving. Don't stop to think. Buy your ticket. Just keep your date book filled with outings, classes, meetings, and trips. Unfortunately, no merry-go-round can spin forever. It stops, and the riders discover they have only circled back to the same lonely spot where they got on. "No matter," the smiling attendant says, "we're here to have fun, not to get anyplace. Buy another ticket. Go around again!" The lure of a more dashing steed, and maybe a gold ring, offers an irresistible proposition. Why not climb on for still another whirl?

Ah, the gold ring, the most deceptive solution of all! "I'll get married, and then I won't be lonely anymore," she says. He, carefully hiding any hint of carnality, says, "Marriage guarantees a loving companion who is always there to share the most profound intimacy two humans can experience. It's physical. It's intellectual. It's spiritual. It's magic."

What Is Loneliness?

Perhaps we're getting ahead of ourselves. We really haven't attempted to discover what loneliness is, or even what causes it. The best way to do this might be to "listen" as singles themselves describe the circumstances of the loneliest moments they can recall. Why don't you join our circle and listen? I've asked a middle-aged woman if she'll start:

"Two and a half years ago my mother died. Soon afterward my father died. Then my marriage broke up. After the funeral the house was so empty it echoed with nothingness."

An attractive blonde says, "I've had hundreds of dates, but I can't find men interested in spiritual things."

"I'm very lonely right now," another middle-aged woman admits. "I'm newly separated, and divorce proceedings have begun."

"I was much lonelier when I was married than I am now," a man confides. A number of heads nod knowingly.

"My most lonely moment," a single mother says, "was the first time my kids went to spend the weekend with their father."

Another says wistfully, "I'm lonely every time I move to a new town."

Loss. Alienation. Isolation. These are the themes common to all these comments. In her book *Beyond Loneliness,* Elizabeth Erlandson distinguishes between positive aspects of aloneness and negative aspects of loneliness. "Aloneness is peaceful and private. Aloneness feels good.

"Loneliness, on the other hand, is quite different. It is not peaceful and does not feel good. It is, rather, a gnawing, aching emptiness that longs for someone who will come and fill it."

Some people grow up lonely, always looking for someone who will fill that aching emptiness within. Others grow lonely after death, distance, or hostility intervenes, and lives that once closely meshed are temporarily or permanently thrown out of gear.

What frightens us is that we, like Adam, can do little about many of the circumstances that produce loneliness. They are at the heart of human experience. Death is sure to separate us from people we love. Some of us never find a mate. Others do and wish they hadn't. Children grow up and leave home. We move to a new city and are separated from familiar surroundings and friends.

There's another dimension of loneliness that's even more profound than our isolation from each other. It's our isolation from God. As St. Augustine said, our hearts *are* restless until we find our rest in God.

But some pious souls (often the ones with successful marriages and dozens of friends) offer doubtful comfort to lonely singles: *"All* you need is God." I think of a gospel song that claims "I'll never be lonely again," because of Jesus' abiding presence. Yes, the Spirit abides in us, but horizontal human relationships and vertical God-human relationships go together; we need both. We need human companionship, someone who will rejoice with us and weep with us. Adam had a relationship with God superior to that of anyone who ever lived, and yet God knew Adam needed something more.

No Other Footprints

When he went down to the river to drink or bathe, Adam always carefully examined the prints of paws and hooves pressed into the muddy bank. *One day,* he thought, *I'll find a mark that matches mine.* Not quite so deep, perhaps. A little finer, maybe. But certainly it would be the imprint of the missing half he was more and more longing to know.

In the animal parade Adam had seen beauty and he had seen absurdity. He had seen the ordinary and the extraordinary. But he had not seen that one *like himself.* No living thing in that long procession (except for some momentary show-offs) walked as he did, let alone looked like him. The others were covered with hair or feathers or scales or shells. *How about some skin?* Adam was thinking.

It was not that he hadn't had a date for two weeks, or that he had tried and been turned down three times in a row. There was *no one* to turn him down. There was *no one* to ask! Every blessed bird and animal and crawling thing had a counterpart, except Adam.

When the heat of another day yielded to the coolness of the Eden evening, Adam bathed and waited. "You don't look too happy, Adam," the voice said.

"I'm tired of talking to the animals."

"I understand perfectly."

"The other night I dreamed ..."

"Would you just listen for a minute? Don't you agree I accomplished quite a lot in six days?"

"People are going to have trouble believing it."

"I think you're right, but you're changing the subject. Each day I could look back and see that what I had done was good. Yes?"

"Yes, Lord, but maybe you should take another look?"

"Adam! Do you think I don't know it's not good, not good at all, that you should be by yourself?"

"You've got the picture, Lord. This definitely won't be a real paradise until I'm a pair."

Sound familiar? Here's the eager, lonely single seeking a like-minded individual of the opposite sex. Genesis 2:18 says that God sent a "helper suitable for" Adam. God knew no animal could ever fulfill this role.

When God Isn't Enough

God knew, too, that even his own presence was not enough, so he provided a flesh-and-blood companion characterized by a physical similarity, an emotional and intellectual similarity. In short, he created two "correspondents" with the potential for intimate relationship at every level.

Just as surely as all of us start life as singles, most of us eventually end up as Adam did. We become half of a pair. In time God may well use marriage as the context for building a relationship that will push loneliness into a far corner of our experience. There is a danger, however. We may impatiently *demand* a mate based on faulty theology. For Adam, the only solution to loneliness may have been a mate. But as sons and daughters of Adam, we have other healthy avenues available as "exits" to loneliness.

I remember a woman I'll call Myrna announcing her ultimatum in response to my asking for prayer requests. "Well, I don't have a prayer request, but if I don't have a husband within thirty days, I'm saying good-bye to church, the Bible, and God."

According to Myrna, marriage was the only possible solution to her needs. She was wrong. Wrong in her assumption and wrong in her demand. A wife was indeed the only possible option for Adam. God's creative work was finished, and he needed subcontractors to build the human race. According to God's plan, that would begin with Adam and Eve. With this once-in-a-universe situation taken care of, another option is open to singles wanting to end loneliness. That option is called friendship.

But often, for any number of reasons, people who are lonely do not reach out to others for fellowship and friendship. Sometimes as miserable as they may be, people draw into themselves, stay home, and lick their wounds. Don't expect these lonely people to turn up at a singles' activity. It seems they would rather be home alone weeping and wailing and gnashing teeth. Sometimes I sense that their loneliness and their pain have become their way of identifying themselves. They ultimately want to be in relationships, but they do not want to take responsibility for finding relationship. It's just easier to stay home and stay safe.

Islands of Isolation

Imagine this rather improbable scene: Three singles are castaways on three small uninhabited islands in the South Pacific. From the beginning the utter isolation produces in each single deep feelings of loneliness. Then one happy day each sees in the distance the other two islands. Smoke from cooking fires tells them other human beings are nearby. Later each single finds an abandoned outrigger canoe has washed up on the beach. (I told you this was improbable.) But each islander looks longingly at the canoe and turns away with a sorrowful complaint: "I'm so lonely I wish I could die."

What's going on here? Why don't these lonely people all pick up a piece of driftwood and start paddling that canoe toward one of the other islands?

Each of these three is miserable, but all are unwilling to take action that could end their isolation. Ask them why they don't launch the canoe and get going. The answer may well be a fearful, "I'm not sure I can get through the waves and currents to one of those other islands." Another castaway may strengthen the argument for inaction: "Besides, what certainty do I have I'll hit it off with whoever is over there?" In other words, these castaways are unwilling to hazard the risks involved to establish a new friendship.

Could that be your problem? I've found passivity to be the most common reason for loneliness among singles.

What may be behind the self-defeating inaction? Fear. The person on Island Alpha has been deeply scarred by relationships involving criticism and rejection. She still hears the echo of a voice that shouted, "I don't love you anymore. Good-bye!" Every slamming door brings back the hurt of those words.

Or she still winces with pain at the memory of the wildflowers she lovingly picked for her mother, only to find them thrown in the trash a few minutes later. As she grew older she gained understanding about her mother's allergies, but the hurt didn't go away. The pain of even one more rejection, she thinks, would be far greater than the pain of life alone on a desert island. She would rather be safe than risk being "shot at."

A second reason paralyzes the single on Island Beta. It may stem from a similar hurt, but pain or fear has turned to anger. "They're all phony-baloneys out there," he says angrily. Hostility and resentment hold his will in an iron grip. They will not allow him to get into a canoe and move toward someone.

Gary Smalley's best-seller giving marital advice, *Making Love Last Forever*, doesn't really get to "marriage" until page 120. The first seven chapters are about "How to Fall in Love with Life." And two of those chapters are about dealing with anger, which he says distances us from others, from God, and even keeps us alienated from our own selves. "One of the most common results or symptoms of deep anger is relational distance, an unwillingness and inability to let others get close. It seems to block our ability to give and receive love." He continues, "Unresolved anger and blame can imprison us and bind us and make us miserable at heart and miserable to live with.... You can break free of unresolved anger. You may need further insight and support to break free, but that freedom is available. And it is a key to staying in love with life and for life."

In her book *Leaving Home*, Evelyn Bence describes an

anger that kept her on a lonely island: "Who *would* I be if I were no longer angry, for my anger, in a sense defined me? Without it I might ... lose my creativity. I might lose my intensity, which I saw as some kind of wall that kept me separated from the rest of the world. I would have to deal with the hole that would be left when the anger vacated. And the size of the hole frightened me."

The third marooned single is a victim of inferiority feelings. Alone with her thoughts on Island Gamma, this person remembers a father's unfavorable comparisons when she was a young girl: "You can't do anything right!" he yelled. She had shown him a spelling test with seven misses out of ten, hoping desperately for help. "I wonder what you'll ever amount to in life," he continued. "Who would ever hire someone like you?" As it turned out, she needed glasses. With corrected vision, her grades improved in all subjects, but the course was set.

Other people whose approval she sought unwittingly communicated the same message of unworthiness. Now she is about as happy as she ever gets, because isolation confirms her self-evaluation: "Who would want to know a nothing like me?"

She will never consciously take action that could result in friendship, for that might prove she were something after all. Such contradictory evidence would be intolerable, so another canoe lies neglected on the beach as the tide goes out once more.

God Knew About Isolation

God loves to move into islands of loneliness like these. He wants to heal the hurt that produced fear and replace it with love. He wants to replace hostility with civility; inferiority with self-worth. He wants these stranded people to get to know one another.

In fact, long before Adam ever arrived on the planet, God anticipated the problem; he did all that needed to be done to end humankind's feeling of alienation. It's the whole thrust of God's plan of redemption. In Ephesians 2 Paul uses words such as "separate," "excluded," and "strangers" to describe a "before" person, who is without "hope and without God in the world." Christ comes on stage and Paul paints an entirely different picture of the "after person," explaining that "you who were formerly far off have been brought near" (Eph 2:13). Now there is oneness. The barriers have been broken down. Enmity is abolished. Reconciliation is a reality. A new life is there. It involves a new relationship with God, and it promises to usher us into relationships with fellow brothers and sisters in Christ. "You are no longer foreigners and aliens, but fellow citizens with God's people and members of God's household" (Eph 2:19), Paul writes, describing the "after" person.

Time for Action

If you are feeling isolated, it's time to make a choice. Will you keep trying to go it alone, or will you let Christ and God's people into the picture? Will you continue to be lonely, or will you take action leading to friendship? Just as you chose to respond to a relationship in fear or anger or inadequacy, you can choose now to deal with hurts and be responsible enough to risk another relationship, regardless of the outcome.

Action involving risk is usually a frightening idea, but it's the heart that pumps life into every aspect of a life lived by faith. I recall one single who admitted at our meeting, "I was lonely, so I came here tonight."

For others such a simple act might constitute very high risk. One evening I got a group activity started at our singles' meeting and stepped outside for a breath of fresh air. A young woman was pacing back and forth nearby. I approached her and found a lonely, frightened woman trying to gain enough courage to open the door and join our group for the first time. With great effort I persuaded her to come in. But she never came back.

Possibly you've known someone like Pete—but then again maybe you haven't! He appeared out of nowhere at one of our singles' meetings. Clearly ill at ease, Pete kept his distance from the others. As the meeting began, I invited him to join the large circle of men and women who had come to share their lives, study, and pray for one another. Pete thanked me, pulled a chair out of the circle, and carried it to the back of the room where he sat down, far from the chatting crowd.

Weeks later I noticed guarded whispers one evening when Pete did join our circle. When his turn came to introduce himself, all he could say was "I pass." It would be many more weeks before the group would hear this desperately lonely man say his name. I do give Pete some credit—at least he had the courage to get out of the house and walk into a room full of potential friends.

The key to understanding loneliness is to know that it isn't the result of circumstances. It's a state of mind. So if you can't change your circumstances, could you change your mind? Why don't we take a brief look at some attitudes that, if changed, could bring the joy of shared laughter into what used to be lonely hours.

If you are alone and lonely because you are too isolated, note these simple ideas that can help you get off dead center and move toward some satisfying relationships.

1. Make friendship, not romance, your goal. In a booklet *How to Overcome Loneliness,* Elisabeth Elliot relates a conversation she had with a seemingly contented single woman named Linda. Linda says she's learned to live without a personal agenda of her own. By that she means she's set aside "thinking there's only one solution [as in 'marriage'], and God has to give you that or nothing." She's set aside "a closed mind," saying that, "A closed mind is a closed heart and a closed door."

This reminds me of Sarah, a young professional who was a bit overweight. Week after week, girlfriends called to invite her to join their activities, but she rebuffed their company, feeling the only solution to her loneliness was a man. After consistent turndowns, the girlfriends stopped calling. Her few male friends hardly ever called, so Sarah spent most weekends at home alone, aiding and abetting her weight problem with potato chips and Twinkies.

2. Don't wait to be invited. Invite! Finally, Sarah became desperate. She put down her half-eaten bag of potato chips, came up with a plan, and took action. As the Romeo of her dreams showed no sign of materializing beneath her balcony, she herself would do the inviting. To do that, she figured she'd have to also invite some girlfriends. (Being desperate, she figured she could do that.) She planned a potluck at her apartment for Sunday after church. She made a list and called ten friends. Not everyone accepted, but that was OK. She had intentionally listed more people than she could easily accommodate. On Sunday Sarah jubilantly welcomed four women and three fellows for what turned out to be the first of many delightful Sunday afternoons. As her real needs—for friendship, companionship, laughter, support—began to be met, Sarah's compulsive eating tapered off.

3. Approach friendships for what you can give, not for what you expect to get. When Sarah could think of nothing but dating, she focused almost exclusively on what she was going to get out of the relationship, not what she could give. Now, as friendships deepened, she saw the needs of others, and she realized she could meet some of these needs. And in so doing she was caught in an upward cycle; helping others was deeply enriching to her own sense of self-worth. One woman, she found, was going through a rough divorce. They decided to meet at a salad bar once a week, have lunch, share, and pray together.

4. Realize that marriage is not a miracle cure for loneliness. As Sarah talked with her friend who was going through divorce, she learned that even the first, best months of marriage could include days of terrible loneliness. As her friend explained one noon, "Marriage promised so much. When it failed to deliver, there was no loneliness to compare with being in the same room or the same bed with someone who wasn't emotionally present." Sarah ruefully admitted she had idealized the marriage relationship, viewing it as the only possible solution for her loneliness.

Remember Pete, the young man who had such a hard time becoming a part of our singles' group? These four principles eventually became a part of Pete's life. Perhaps in response to the love he experienced in some very humbling personal encounters, Pete found Christ as his Savior. And in time he was delightfully surprised at his ability to move into healthy friendships.

How would you rate your loneliness quotient on a scale of one to five, one being utterly content and five being utterly dysfunctional?

Chances are you're not like Pete, who could not speak his name in a group setting. In all probability, you're a two or a three—functioning within some social norms. But what can you do to loosen the grip loneliness has on you?

Is a little smile beginning to turn up the corners of your mouth now that you know God was able to provide Adam with companionship? God even had a way out for Pete. Will you trust God to provide an escape for you? If he does, will you take it?

A few themes addressed in this first chapter will come up again in subsequent chapters. In chapter two we'll look at Hagar and her struggle with rejection. Later we'll consider important elements of friendship in the lives of Mary and Martha.

The Second Mile

1. List words you might include in a definition of loneliness.
2. How do you think the loneliness experienced today compares to the intensity of loneliness experienced by Adam?
3. How would you explain to someone that promiscuity or a calendar full of activities cannot be expected to solve the problem of loneliness?
4. Evaluate marriage as a guaranteed cure for loneliness.
5. If your lack of relationships and consequent loneliness are a result of passivity, what practical steps could you take that would bring people into your life?
6. What relationship do you see between loneliness and our closeness to God?
7. Would you advise a single friend to seek friendship rather than romance as an escape from loneliness? Why?
8. The three singles improbably stranded on separate islands were unable to initiate relationships because of fear, anger, and feelings of unworthiness. Of these three, with which do you struggle the most? Give an example of one time when this internal struggle kept you from reaching out to a potential friend.
9. Read Ephesians 2. Start two columns on a piece of paper and head them "Before" and "After." In the first column, write down all the words that characterize alienation from God. In the second, list key words that describe our new relationship after redemption.
10. Which column describes your relationship to God right now? If you see yourself being in column 1, what does God want you to do to move to column 2?

you can't play on my team, kid

Hagar: A Rejected Single Parent
Who Discovered God's Care

For the story of Hagar, see Genesis 16 and 21.

Waiting for the doors to open at a downtown bank, Carla perused the people around her. She particularly noticed an elegantly dressed man, maybe fifty years old, with an unusual mustache. Passing the time visiting with others in the line, she knew the man with the mustache kept looking at her. Suddenly the big doors swung open and people hurried in.

Carla saw the man with the mustache again, in a different line from the one she was in. She thought she heard a teller call the man "Paul," but she couldn't be sure.

Later, to take care of other transactions, Carla and the mustached man both stood in the same line, with just two people between them. Carla caught him staring at her several times, and she studied him from this closer vantage point: his glasses, his mannerisms, his clothes, and especially the ring on his left hand. She was almost sure she knew who he was, but she forced back the powerful emotions that were flooding her heart.

When she heard the man's voice and saw the easy way he joked with the teller, Carla was sure. It was Paul, her Paul. The man who ...

The teller called her name. The man with the mustache walked by her, but she couldn't bring herself to speak. She stumbled to the counter and with trembling hands took the crisp bills the teller counted out.

Paul. They'd met twenty-three years earlier, at the beach. They'd gone together for a year and became engaged. Then, having second thoughts, Carla had called it off. The next day, sure she'd made a terrible mistake, she had tried to reverse her decision. Paul had said no, it was over. She was sure he was too proud to take back the woman who had rejected him.

Heartbroken, she couldn't stop loving him, and she was certain that someday they would marry.

Two years later Carla heard that Paul had been badly hurt in a car accident. When he was released from the hospital, Carla went to his home to care for him. Surely this demonstration of her love would restore their relationship.

But at the end of a week, a young woman appeared and said she was Paul's fiancée. The shock of losing Paul again was more than Carla could bear. She landed in a psychiatric ward, diagnosed as manic depressive. Once released, she still wasn't doing very well. Hoping to resolve the issue and help her regain her health, her well-meaning parents told her Paul had died.

Now a middle-aged woman, Carla left the bank confused and disoriented. *He's not dead. My parents lied to me.* She waited for a subway train, thinking, *What was I supposed to say to him? Congratulations? You triggered the psychotic disorder I've struggled with all these years?*

She remembered her frequent trips to the doctor, the daily medication, the friends who didn't always understand her. Carla relived a scenario of rejection, even betrayal. She couldn't hate Paul—or her parents. She had good reason not to be bitter. She knew God had used the situation and her inability to cope to bring her to Christ. And yet the wound of rejection still stung terribly.

And had perhaps God rejected her too? After all, he never had given her a husband.

The Reality of Rejection

Rejection is a reality we all experience. For me it started in childhood. Someone told me I looked funny without my two front teeth, and I tried to stop smiling. Then my friends would choose up sides for baseball, and I (hardly a major leaguer) was always among the last to be chosen. In high school, because I was a Christian, I chose not to participate in the questionable activities of my classmates. "What's the matter with you?" my friend Johnny said crossly one day. "Are you going to be a stick-in-the-mud all your life?" The words of rejection cut, and the pain lingers.

Then one day you're grown up. It's time to apply for a job. You are the most qualified of three finalists, but one of the other two gets the call. Or you find that certain someone and start to talk about a permanent relationship. "I don't think so," Certain Someone says. Later Certain Someone Else breathes an ecstatic yes. Three kids and twenty-four years later, that spouse says, "There's someone else in my life—younger, better looking, more fun, more exciting." Or, "I can't live with you any-more. I need my space."

The years roll by, and the time comes when it's increasingly hard to get out of your recliner. You don't drive anymore, and getting through the day is more than you can handle alone. "Dad," your daughter tells you, "I know our kids are gone and we have all that extra space, but you know how we're on the go all the time. I'm sorry, but we're going to have to put you in a home."

Bit Player With a Starring Role

We never expected life to be like that, and neither did Hagar. She was the young woman from Egypt who became Sarai's maid. You can read all about her in Genesis 16 and 21. Well, not *all* about her, because we don't know exactly how she came into Abram and Sarai's lives, though we do know Abram and Sarai spent some time in Egypt once to escape famine.

One thing we do know for sure. Hagar, this apparently insignificant Egyptian servant, was to play a major role in world history. Let me recap how it all started. God repeatedly promised old Abram that he was going to have a son. Old Abram? Yes. He was seventy-five. He had been married about fifty years to barren Sarai, and they were in Canaan waiting for God to fulfill his promise of a son.

The years ticked by. Five, ten, fifteen. After twenty-four years God seemed to have forgotten all about his astonishing promise. I imagine Abram might have been just dozing off one night when Sarai rolled over and shook his shoulder. "Abe, wake up. Did God ever say anything about my being the mother of the son he promised?"

"The what?"

"The son Jehovah said he's going to give you. Did he say anything about my being the mother?"

"Well, now that you mention it, I guess he didn't. I'm to be the father, so I just assumed …"

"There you go again, taking God for granted. Listen, Abe, have I got a plan for you!"

God Needs Help?

Sarai's plan was based on the notion that God was in trouble and needed a little help to get his program off the ground. She suggested that Abram have a child by Hagar. Today we give Sarai's plan a fancy name. We call it surrogate motherhood. Modern techniques of impregnation are impersonal and extremely sophisticated, but the results sometimes seem as disastrous as this ménage à trois.

The trouble began almost immediately. The maid's dislike for her mistress seemed to grow in direct proportion to the swelling of her Egyptian belly. You can understand something of what lay behind Hagar's disdain for Sarai if you remember that barrenness in Old Testament times was considered a curse or punishment from God. Fecundity, on the other hand, was a sure sign of God's blessing.

As a man, I say Sarai reacted to Hagar's insolence in predictable fashion: She blamed her husband. "You are responsible for the wrong I am suffering. I put my servant in your arms, and now that she knows she is pregnant, she despises me. May the Lord judge between you and me" (Gn 16:5).

So Hagar rejected Sarai, and Sarai returned the favor. Abram wanted no part of it. "Do with her whatever you think best," he said passively (v. 6).

I can hear someone saying, "Abram, I can't believe you said that! Hagar is carrying your child. Can't you guess what Sarai is going to do to her? This is a desperate situation, and your willingness to intervene is crucial! Otherwise, you're rejecting the woman God will use to fulfill his promise to make from you a great nation called Israel."

That was not the case, of course, but at this point in the story Abram must have thought that Hagar's child would be his only child. (In Genesis 17 God told Abram that the son of promise was yet to be born and that Sarai would be his mother.) No matter. The stage at this point was set for a tragedy of epic proportions.

Fight or Flight?

What's your usual response to rejection? Derek Prince, in *God's Remedy for Rejection,* says there are at least three possibilities: give in, hold out, or fight back. It seems Hagar seriously looked only at two: fight or give in. Her situation seemed hopeless, beyond resolution, so she gave in and ran away. How could she do otherwise? Sarai, the woman she had faithfully served all these years, was abusing her verbally and perhaps even physically. In addition, the man who fathered her child had turned out to be a spineless wimp who refused to intervene on her behalf.

In response to this double whammy, Hagar ran away, heading for Egypt. Pregnant, unmarried, and despised by the two people who should have loved her most, there was no longer a future for her in Canaan. Did more rejection, the rejection of friends and family, await her in Egypt? *I can't take any more rejection,* she thought as she wearily sank down beside a desert spring to drink and rest. *But what other choice do I have?*

In his book *Finding God in the Dark,* David Walls recounts a preacher's advice, which Hagar needed to hear at this stage. "When God has you in His vice, you can kick and scream all you want, but He will not let you free until He has finished what He is doing in your life." Maybe some of us also need to let those words sink in.

Or perhaps not. Perhaps you've already learned the great spiritual lessons Hagar was about to learn. Lesson 1: God is a God who sees. He is aware when the pain of rejection becomes unbearable and we're out of gas physically, emotionally, and spiritually. Lesson 2: God has a way of challenging us to tackle tough, unexpected assignments, especially when we experience rejection. For people like Hagar who give up and run away, Derek Prince sees an awful chain of destructive results that follow rejection that is not dealt with: loneliness, self-pity, misery, depression, despair, and even suicide. Will you let these negative emotions overwhelm your life? Or will you make the choices only you can make to move forward?

Touched by an Angel

The second half of Genesis 16 records extraordinary events surrounding the choices made by a rejected, single mother-to-be.

We are told that the "angel of the Lord" found Hagar sitting by the spring on the road to Shur. The appearance of this angel may not seem quite so remarkable if I explain that this is but one occurrence of a phenomenon surprisingly common in the Old Testament.

This "angel of the Lord," "angel of God," or "angel of his presence," as he is sometimes called, is mentioned more than twenty times. His description, acts, and attributes are a fascinating study too extended to include here. Suffice it to say, most Bible scholars feel this mysterious person is a *theophany*, a member of the Trinity, a temporary appearance of the Messiah, the Logos—Jesus Christ. Even this single passage gives strong hints that this "angel" was omnipresent and omniscient.

What a wonderful time for Jesus to put in an appearance! The people who were most important to Hagar had rejected her. Her future back home in Egypt as a single mother—if she were to make it—was uncertain. Here was someone who noticed her and accepted her for what she was. He knew her name, knew whom she worked for, knew she was pregnant, and was concerned about her welfare. He approached her with a gentleness she hadn't experienced for a long, long time.

"What in the world are you doing out here in the desert, Hagar?"

"I'm running away from my awful, hateful mistress."

"Beautiful Sarai? Hateful?"

"Yes, because I'm going to have a baby and she's not."

"So I see. And are there any other reasons why she might hate you?"

"Well, I guess I got a little cheeky when I knew I was pregnant."

"True enough. You actually despised your mistress, isn't that right?"

"Well, what was I supposed to do? I did what she wanted. I gave her what she wanted. And all the thanks I got was to get kicked around and thrown out!"

We can't actually know all the words that passed between Hagar and the angel. The account is disturbingly brief, but there is refreshing honesty in Hagar's answer, "I'm running away from my mistress, Sarai" (v. 8). Honesty is always the first step for letting God get us back on track when we experience rejection.

We could wish some obvious New Testament concepts were included at this point. How about forgiveness? Doesn't Hagar have to forgive the man who refused to defend her and the woman who made life so intolerable that she risked her life on a long, lonely trip home?

Yes, I think there has to be forgiveness. I find no other explanation for Hagar's decision to obey the angel's instruction to her to turn around and go back to Sarai's tent.

Sometimes the agony life dishes up seems to mock everything we believe about ourselves and about God. Would Jesus really say something like that? Go back to that brawling family where rejection will continue, maybe as an everyday, ongoing reality? Go back to that hellish household? Yes, he sometimes says strange things like that. But when he knows he's asking the near impossible, he's always there with all the encouragement we need. This encouragement is embodied in several remarkably detailed statements that can be summarized in just three lines:

1. God is aware of human misery, including the misery of rejection.
2. He knows just the right time and the right way to intervene.
3. Nothing can thwart his final purpose.

Let's look just for a minute at that first principle. When Christ meets us on our road to Shur, we can be sure of one thing: He understands rejection. His very own family thought he was crazy (see Mk 3:20-21). Later in John 7, when Jesus was avoiding Judea to escape plots against his life, not even his brothers believed he was the Christ (see Jn 7:5). Near the end of his ministry, one from his chosen circle of twelve turned him over to the enemy. Then Peter, one of the three men closest to Jesus, the man who had said, "I'll go to prison or even to death with you," denied even being acquainted with him (see Lk 22:56-61). Finally, after ministering for almost three years under the constant threat of death, Jesus was killed in the ultimate demonstration of rejection. Truly, if any man understood rejection, it was Jesus. Isaiah 53:3 describes it well:

> He was despised and rejected by men,
>> a man of sorrows, and familiar with suffering.
> Like one from whom men hide their faces
>> he was despised, and we esteemed him not.

Tough Decision

What would be your response to God's presence and his understanding that Hagar experienced? Scripture says, "She gave this name to the Lord who spoke to her: 'You are the God who sees me,' for she said, 'I have now seen the One who sees me'" (vv. 11-13).

Something about what she had seen in that One motivated her to choose to obey his command. I expect she saw and sensed God's loving, tender mercies. And when God saw her, he knew what she most needed was acceptance—his acceptance. The only acceptance that really counts. Perhaps you remember when you first realized that God loved you even though you had rejected him. It is his nature to love and accept you through the relationship you established with his Son. I like the way Paul explains what happens:

> God ... reconciled us to himself through Christ and gave us the ministry of reconciliation: that God was reconciling the world to himself in Christ, not counting men's sins against them. And he has committed to us the message of reconciliation. We are therefore Christ's ambassadors, as though God were making his appeal through us. We implore you on Christ's behalf: Be reconciled to God. God made him who had no sin to be sin for us, so that in him we might become the righteousness of God.
>
> 2 CORINTHIANS 5:18-21

Now *that's* acceptance. Understanding what it means to be "accepted in the beloved" has been crucial to my spiritual growth. It was the only thing that got me through several experiences when I was rejected by people whose approval I thought was crucial to my survival.

Have you learned this powerful lesson of survival in times of rejection? Paul, a man who knew quite a bit about rejection, grasped this truth and wrote, "If God is for us, who can be against us?" (Rom 8:31). Can you imagine a circumstance when God would not be for you? Paul's "if" could just as well be translated "in view of the fact that," or "since." And Jesus, who suffered the ultimate rejection, was able to say, "Father, forgive them, for they do not know what they are doing" (Lk 23:34).

I don't know if Hagar was able to say that about Sarai and Abram, but she did go back to Sarai's tent. I think the decision was one of the most difficult Hagar ever made. Here she was, a pagan idolater not exposed to the most positive model of what a godly life is all about, doing what God told her to do. Obedience is never easy, regardless of the encouragement God gives us. We don't like it; we don't understand it. In his book *When Your Rope Breaks*, Stephen Brown calls obedience "positive relinquishment."

Jesus said: "Why do you call me, 'Lord, Lord,' and do not do what I say? I will show you what he is like who comes to me and hears my words and puts them into practice. He is like a man building a house, who dug down deep and laid the foundation on rock. When a flood came, the torrent struck that house but could not shake it, because it was well built" (Lk 6:46-48). The purpose of obedience is not to make us miserable, but to give us freedom and security.

God Owes You One?

What thoughts do you suppose were going through Hagar's mind as she turned and headed back down the road toward

Abram's encampment? If she were a contemporary Christian, she might be saying to herself, *I'm paying a terrible price to step out on faith and obey. Can I forgive Sarai? Have I forgiven her? However you cut it, I'm going back, and God owes me one. Certainly he will reward me by resolving the problem I ran from; he'll resolve it even before I get back.*

Well, Hagar wasn't a contemporary Christian, but even with her limited knowledge of God, I believe she was far more realistic about her future than we might be under similar circumstances. Because the angel was sending her back, she knew running away was not her answer. It may have logically followed that God wanted her to go back and confront Sarai's hatred and challenge Abram's lack of concern for her and his child. How else would she have the security she needed to bear and rear what the angel called this "wild donkey of a man" (v. 12)?

We aren't told *how* Hagar worked things out when she returned, but apparently she did. Baby Ishmael arrived, I imagine bellowing so loudly the whole camp knew he'd come into the world safe and sound. Eighty-six-year-old Abram recognized the boy as his son, gave him the name indicated by the angel, and loved him.

Seeing the God Who Sees

I expect that Abram and Sarai sensed a difference in Hagar—after she had seen the angel of the Lord. I can imagine Sarai thinking, if not saying, "Hagar, there's something different about you...."

"How can I not be different? I saw the God who saw me!"

Perhaps the first step you need to take in restoring a relationship in which you feel rejected is to meet God face to face, hear his voice, obey his commands. Your attitude, to say the least, will be different and people will know it. Remember the old adage: To change others, change yourself. Better still, let an encounter with the living God change you so others will change.

Returning to Hagar's story: Fifteen years passed. Ishmael, now in his midteens, was about to get a half brother. The God who saw Hagar also saw Sarai, her mistress. Isaac, the son of promise, was born to ninety-year-old Sarai (now Sarah). She looked over at her hundred-year-old husband, now called Abraham, laughed, and said, "I have borne him a son in *his* old age" (Gn 21:7, emphasis mine).

Everyone looked over at beaming Abraham and laughed. Then they all laughed again with Sarah at the wonder of one of God's great miracles. But I wonder: Was Hagar laughing? Did she remember the angel's prophecy about her son? "His hand will be against everyone and everyone's hand against him, and he will live in hostility toward all his brothers" (Gn 16:12). This stubborn, self-willed teenager had a brother now. It appeared that another crisis might be just around the corner. *Have you grown in your walk with God, Hagar? Are you ready for a another big one? Can you handle more rejection?*

Who Hit the Replay Button?

Three, four, maybe even five years passed. Isaac was weaned. Waiting for this day with great anticipation, Abraham threw a major party. Ishmael, now in his late teens, was there, watching little Isaac toddle around, responding to the adoring attention of the party-goers. Ishmael couldn't stand the little brat. "Everyone thinks he's so cute, and they're spoiling him rotten," he sneered.

Instantly Sarah called her husband over to a corner of the tent. "Get rid of that slave woman and her son, for that slave woman's son will never share in the inheritance of my son Isaac" (Gn 21:10).

The savage cycle of rejection was set in motion all over again. It was no longer Hagar, but "that slave woman." It's not Ishmael, Abraham's child, but "her son."

Abraham was deeply troubled. How could he send them away? He had previously poured out his heart before God for that child, praying: "If only Ishmael might live under your blessing!" (Gn 17:18). Hearing his prayer, God had promised the blessing, giving him a prophetic glimpse of the great nation Ishmael would become. But here God told Abraham to listen to his wife, do what she said. Under these new circumstances, flight was the only way to save Hagar and her son.

This time Hagar didn't know where to go. God had promised something very special for the future of her very special son. How was he going to accomplish his purpose now? Without direction, she wandered through the desert of Beersheba. Soon the food Abraham had given them was gone. Then the water skin was empty. *Did Abraham give us short rations thinking we would be forced to return?* Hagar may have thought, but it seemed to be too late. Ishmael collapsed. His mother rolled him under the shade of some desert bushes, walked a short distance away, sat down, and sobbed.

I can't watch my boy die. Where are you, God? That's the father of a great nation over there. Don't you see what's happening? (See Gn 21:14-16.)

"The greater the trial, the more intense the pain. The greater the pain, the more we tend to question God's purpose," notes Christian psychiatrist Joel A. Freeman in his book *God Is Not Fair.*

The God Who Hears

This time God's intervention was all audio. It's not noted that God *saw*. He *heard*. He heard the sobbing of a dehydrated, dying boy to whom he had promised greatness. And this time the angel of the Lord didn't appear. He spoke to Hagar from heaven. "Don't be afraid…. Lift the boy up and take him by the hand" (Gn 21:17-18).

In a tremendous leap of faith, Hagar disregarded everything her mind was telling her. I can imagine her thinking, *Are you crazy? Let the boy die in peace. Leave him alone!* Once again, she found the strength to do what God told her to do. And then she found out why God wanted Ishmael in a sitting position. Her eyes "opened," and she saw a well nearby. Water, God's provision for their future, was at hand. The boy revived as Hagar herself "went and filled the skin with water and gave the boy a drink" (v. 19). God provided the water. Can you imagine Hagar not running to appropriate God's provision? Why is it so difficult for us to appropriate the grace he supplies, accept it, and make it our own?

We have no indication that Hagar ever saw Sarah or

Abraham again. Given the circumstances, reconciliation seems highly unlikely. What was Hagar to do? Would she live the rest of her life under this suffocating cloud of rejection? The record doesn't tell us, but it's clear Hagar had the same two options we have when people push us out of their lives. We can forgive. Or we can bottle up the pain and let its vitriolic churning turn us into bitter and angry people.

But doesn't the other person have to ask to be forgiven? There are many references in the New Testament (see Mk 11:25, for example) that talk of granting forgiveness but require neither the request nor the repentance of the offender. Probably the best example is given in Luke 23:34, where Christ asked God to forgive those responsible for crucifying him. Could they ask for forgiveness? Jesus indicated they had no idea what they were doing.

To forgive or not to forgive? Which option will you exercise? It's almost a no-brainer, when we realize that in some mysterious way God forgives us on the basis of how we forgive those who sin against us (see Mt 6:12-15).

The God Who Heals

Hagar had distanced herself from the people who wounded her so deeply. God had spared her and her son from death in a hostile desert. And now, after twice giving a similar message to Abraham, God told Hagar directly that this boy recovering from dehydration would become the father of a great nation. It was time for the healing process to begin—time for Hagar to get on with her life and watch God give substance to his incredible promise. Hagar established a home, found a bride from Egypt for Ishmael, and one by one the tribal heads of this new nation were born.

Has the time for healing come for you? You've done all you can. The hurt is deep, and reconciliation is impossible. Let God show you it's time to move on and begin the healing process. Let him lead you to rest in green pastures and beside quiet waters. Let him restore your soul as he guides you in paths of righteousness for his name's sake (see Ps 23:2-3).

Go Figure

Perhaps you've already learned more than you bargained for from Hagar's experience, but there's more. Let's check out six additional principles.

1. Improved circumstances can bring new temptations. More money, more prestige, more leisure time—it all sounds very nice. For Hagar, in her culture, having a child "on behalf of" her mistress might have sounded like a great opportunity. But, once pregnant, Hagar couldn't keep her attitude toward Sarai in check. If things get better for you, pray that God will help you keep your balance.

2. It's easy to do foolish things under stress. When my M.D. brother-in-law worked for NASA, he developed a device to measure an astronaut's ability to perform simple and complex tasks under stress. No one was very surprised to discover that the greater the stress level, the poorer the ability to think and act.

Perhaps that quiet time Hagar had in her first desert "retreat" was crucial for her to be able to hear God's voice and change her attitude. In the face of rejection, we might see fight or flight as our only two options, but are they really? (Seek more insight below, in "The Second Mile" section.) I'm not suggesting that either confronting or running from a painful circumstance is always foolish or misguided. God directs in different ways depending upon the situation. Are you listening for that direction? Are you daily praying for that direction?

3. A God who sees and hears is also able to meet our every need. Discovering the reality of a living God might have had greater impact on an idolater than on us who find the Egyptian pantheon only a curiosity. But a God who sees and hears is a personal God, a caring God. Psalm 94:7-9 challenges those who don't believe this.

> They say, "The Lord does not see;
> > the God of Jacob pays no heed."
> Take heed, you senseless ones among the people;
> > you fools, when will you become wise?
> Does he who implanted the ear not hear?
> Does he who formed the eye not see?

Those of us who know Hagar's personal God are blessed every time we rediscover this revolutionary truth. He sees. He hears.

4. God has a divine purpose for each of our lives. An angel of the Lord may not appear to you and give you cryptic details, as he did Hagar, but be assured that you are a special person whom God is going to use in a way he will use no one else.

Many years ago as we were preparing to return to Brazil, my wife grew very discouraged. "How is God going to use someone like me?" she asked. She felt her time spent in home schooling would curtail ministry opportunities.

I tried to encourage her, but the real encouragement came from the Lord. She read that evangelist Billy Graham was about to hold one of his crusades in Rio's giant Maracanã Stadium. Hundreds of thousands would come to hear him. Then she realized that not even Billy Graham would be able to reach the people God would bring to Christ through her witness. Would Billy push our dimpled, blond toddler up and down the street? No, but Julie did. Her "stroller evangelism" was instrumental in bringing a whole family to Christ. A Sunday school began that today is a thriving church. In addition, a teenager from that family is now a mature woman with three hundred students enrolled in her Christian school. The prophet Jeremiah would not have been surprised, for he wrote, "'For I know the plans I have for you,' declares the Lord, 'plans to prosper you and not to harm you, plans to give you hope and a future'" (Jer 29:11).

5. The methods God uses to accomplish his will sometimes seem harsh. As a single grandmother, Hagar must have looked back at those terrible days with Sarah and remembered the pain of being pushed into God's mold. Then, as she bounced a couple of Ishmael's kids on her knee, she knew it was all worth it. If you're a single mother, perhaps this is, or may be, God's reward for your faithfulness. If not, think through your life right now and pick the blessing that most makes you give thanks for the difficult days when God was stretching and shaping you to be like his Son.

Today we're in such a hurry to get where God wants us. And we want to get there without hurts, conflict, hard choices, or disappointment. Yes, God does sometimes get a little rough. Perhaps you've noticed it often seems in direct proportion to our ability to hear his voice and submit to the transformation he wants to bring about in us. As I write I'm going through a kind of spiritual boot camp. Loving friends and the constant reminder of God's love help me see that he "disciplines us for our good, that we may share in his holiness" (Heb 12:10).

6. When we are rejected by people who should love us, God's strength, comfort, and encouragement are always there. Hagar shared her first desert experience of rejection with an unborn child; her second as the single mother of a teenager. In both cases her son was an encumbrance, not a help. But God was there to accept her, guide her, and encourage her in the midst of her helplessness and hopelessness. Have you ever wondered what to do when one extra burden made the difficult seem impossible?

In 1895 while traveling far from home, Andrew Murray, whose devotional writings have become classic favorites, was suffering nearly unbearable back pain from an old injury. One morning his hostess told him of a woman downstairs who was in great trouble; she wanted to know if he had any advice for her. Murray handed over the paper on which he had been writing advice for himself. He thought she might find it helpful:

In this time of trouble, say, "First, He brought me here. It is by His will I am in this strait place, in that I will rest." Next, "He will keep me here in His love, and give me grace in this trial to behave as His child." Then say, "He will make the trial a blessing, teaching me lessons He intends me to learn, and working in the grace He means to bestow." And last, say, "In His good time He can bring me out again. How and when, He knows." Therefore, say, "I am here (1) by God's appointment, (2) in his keeping, (3) under His training, (4) for His time."

When you face rejection, will you look for God's direction, and obey no matter how hard it is? Will you stay or go as he indicates? Will you love him enough to struggle through forgiveness, knowing he forgave you of so much before you even asked?

The Second Mile

1. What is the most painful rejection you suffered as a child, adolescent, adult?
2. Does rejection press you closer to God or drive you away? Why?
3. Psalm 55 suggests at least four ways to handle rejection. Read the psalm and identify as many as you can find.
4. To which of the Psalm 55 methods of dealing with rejection do you most easily resort?
5. Which of the methods has proven to be most effective in the long run?
6. Look at your life and identify one currently broken relation-

ship. What can you do that will help you walk toward healing of your own heart?

7. Discuss or in a journal write your response to this quote from *She Can Laugh at the Days to Come* by Valerie Bell:

> I am not a woman who is conformed to my pain, whose self-definition is the litany of sins that has been committed against me…. No. I am a woman whose soul is forming to God. I cannot control how others treat me, but I can control my own response. I choose to relate to others based on my own character, not theirs…. My soul, formed in its "becoming" to the dimensions of God's love, can extend forgiveness, even when the other person is not worthy, never says the word "sorry," or ever shows a grain of remorse.

all stressed up and no place to grow?

Joseph: The Single Who Knew What to Do With Stress

For the story of Joseph, see Genesis 37, 39-41.

Over the course of just a few months, Eddie's good life crumbled. His wife moved out and filed for divorce. He was forbidden to see their kids. Things couldn't get much worse? They did. He lost his job, and soon afterward his mother died. Struggling against the riptide of incredible stress, Eddie sat on the edge of his bed one night, unable to sleep. He took his .45 pistol out of the nightstand drawer. Fingering the safety catch, he asked aloud: "There must be a way out. I wonder if this is it?"

Perhaps you can identify with Eddie. You, too, know about stress. You've lost good things. As if that weren't enough, bad things muscled in to take their places. Dreams crashed. A promotion at work was offered, only to be retracted. You're not always thinking clearly, and you've been sick more than usual. You sometimes feel even one more change may tip you beyond the point of no return.

T.H. Holmes and R.H. Rahe, two professors at the

University of Washington, teamed up to study stress. They found that change in itself, whether for good or bad, produces stress. Stressed out, we are susceptible to disease, and our thinking processes are impaired. In other words, it's a good time to get sick and a bad time to make major decisions. Look at the top ten from the Holmes and Rahe list of forty stress-producing events, published in the *Journal of Psychosomatic Research* in 1967.

1. Death of a spouse

2. Divorce

3. Marital separation

4. Jail term

5. Death of a close family member

6. Personal injury or illness

7. Marriage

8. Fired at work

9. Marital reconciliation

10. Retirement

They're not all bad, are they? In fact, numbers 7, 9, and 10 are quite positive. But they all cut through the routines of life and put us on wide-eyed alert.

I think Joseph, the eleventh son of patriarch Jacob, would have understood these modern ideas about change-induced stress. He was one of those singles who had more ups and downs than a finalist pumping through the last day of the world championship yo-yo competition. Look at the pressures this seventeen-year-old was under at home when we first hear about him in Genesis 37. He's a responsible son coming in to tell his father, Jacob, that Joseph's brothers aren't tending to business. The father's response? "You've done well, son, and I love you very much. Here's a present I've been saving. It's only a coat, but I had it especially decorated just for you."

How did you feel as a teenager when your dad did something special for you? Joseph was on top of the world. Then at supper his brothers came in and saw this blatant evidence of parental favoritism. "Dad loves you more than all of us, you disgusting little creep," one of them said. "We hate your guts, and we're going to remind you every chance we get." Joseph had been up, but now he was down, crushed by his older brothers' intense loathing. Was it Joseph's fault his father was trying to spoil him?

Stress at Home

Then one night, sleeping, Joseph dreamt that his sheaf of wheat in the field stood straight and tall while his brothers' sheaves bowed to it. It seems Joseph sensed the dream was from God, and it seemed his family would somehow be subject to his authority. He was so excited, he couldn't go back to sleep. He sat up, trembling. "God is sharing his secrets with *me*," he whispered. "He's chosen to use *me* in a special way." In the morning Joseph shared the dream with his family. His brothers mocked him and "hated him all the more" (Gn 37:8).

Then Joseph had a second dream: "The sun and moon and eleven stars were bowing down to me" (v. 9). Again, he rather foolishly bragged of his dream to his family. This time even his father "rebuked" him, and then silently mulled over the matter.

Get the picture? Up, down, up, down. Loving acceptance, then rejection. Assurances of success, followed by failure. If you drew a line graph of the stress Joseph experienced in the first thirty years of his life, it would resemble the Cal Tech seismographic record of a 6.5 quake, including all the aftershocks. Genesis 37 tells us about the incidents in the stressful, unstable, home life of young Joseph:

Up: Dad trusts him to evaluate his brothers and report on them.

Down: Brothers hate the tattletale.

Up: Father shows love with a special coat.

Down: Brothers show more hatred for Dad's pet.

Up: God reveals wonderful news to Joseph in a dream.

Down: Incredulity and more hatred from family.

Up: God confirms his message in a second dream.

Down: Dad rebukes Joseph, and brothers are jealous.

Up: Joseph goes to visit the shepherding brothers in obedience to Dad.

Down: The brothers plot to kill Joseph, but instead throw him in a dry well and then sell him to traveling merchants as a slave. They dip his colorful coat in goat's blood, present it to their father, and say Joseph must have been killed by some ferocious wild animal.

Perhaps you know a young person whose life is characterized by these kinds of wrenching emotional flip-flops. You've observed his or her response to these situations, and you're ready to announce your conclusions about Joseph: "I'm sorry to have to tell you that he will grow up to be an angry, bitter, judgmental, and disillusioned man."

But that's not how the story ends. Joseph did not end up bitter and disillusioned. Somehow every stressful change—whether for better or worse—only served to build into Joseph spiritual balance, strength, and resolve. These are the qualities we would love to see in our own lives. How did he do that? What was this remarkable young man's secret?

Stress at Work

To discover Joseph's secret for using stress positively as a tool for growth, we should track him through his young adult years. Far from home, Joseph became a slave in Egypt. Genesis 39 tells the next chapter of the up-and-down story of college-age Joseph.

Up: Has privilege and honor of favorite son.
Down: Loses everything in slavery.

Up: Master, named Potiphar, knows talent when he sees it and makes Joseph his CEO.
Down: Joseph fends off the advances of his boss's overheated wife. But he loses his cloak in the fracas.

Up: Enormous satisfaction of resisting the irresistible. Boss will be pleased.

Down: Boss believes wife's trumped-up charge of sexual assault. (The torn coat she has looks like damning evidence.) He sends Joseph to prison.

With these developments at Potiphar's house, it would appear that every change was taking Joseph a little further down. So far he's retrogressed from favored son to slave to convict. How did he handle the stress that rejection produces? By getting bitter and cynical? How do you respond emotionally to the stress of undeserved reverses?

Dreams Do Come True

Genesis 39–41 chronicles Joseph's continuing life of stress. He didn't pass go. He didn't collect two hundred shekels. He went straight to jail and a brand-new set of ups and downs. By now he's about twenty-seven. Here's what I think Joseph must have been thinking as he peered through the bars:

Up: Finally! I'm safe from the clutches of that horrible woman.

Down: This place sure is cold without any kind of coat.

Up: The warden is taking a liking to me.

Down: It looks like I may be in here for a long while.

Up: The jail keeper likes me. He's made me second in command of this prison.

Down: Two new prisoners, banished from the palace, are really depressed today.

Up: These men had dreams, and I can explain what they mean.

Down: I'm going to have to give the baker some very bad news.

Up: Pharaoh's cup bearer is out of prison, and he said he'll put in a good word with Pharaoh, try to get me released.

Down: It's been two full years. How could that rascal forget me?

Up: Pharaoh is calling for me to come and see him.

Down: Pharaoh had a dream. I can interpret it, but it's bad news, and I hear he has a temper.

Up: Pharaoh was impressed rather than distressed. He's asked me to become his prime minister.

Down: What's going to become of this little Jewish shepherd boy now?

Despite the stressful ups and downs, in just thirteen years Joseph had pole-vaulted from a sheepherder in Canaan to the prime minister of Egypt. Pharaoh installed this thirty-year-old marvel in office with great fanfare. Joseph married Asenath, an upper-class local girl. He began a career that would be characterized by one brilliant administrative feat after another. The job brought rewards, but of course a position of that stature was itself extremely stressful. And ahead of him he faced a series of incredibly tense family gatherings that would tear his heart in two. But we won't follow Joseph's entire story, after his marriage. (You can review it by reading Genesis 42–50.)

We already have more than enough information to answer the question we posed in the beginning. What was the secret that enabled Joseph to manage stress in such a way that it could be a positive element for growth?

Like a silver thread, a little phrase is woven repeatedly into the amazingly detailed Old Testament narrative of Joseph: "The Lord was with Joseph." The words first occur in Genesis 39:2, to indicate God's blessing on Joseph's emerging administrative abilities in Potiphar's household. And although it's not explicitly stated, God was certainly with Joseph even during his troubled years at home, as there God spoke to him in two dreams.

Let's Ask Joseph

This phrase, "The Lord was with Joseph," appears at least three more times. Someone's trying to get our attention. What did these five words mean to Joseph as he faced stress? If you allow me to use a little imagination—OK, a lot of imagination, including a time warp—perhaps we can gain some insights from Joseph himself.

JIM: Joe, you're a fellow who seems to have a hard time keeping track of his coats. Is that right?

JOE: I did have my problems with coats. I laugh about it now sometimes, but I still remember those two traumatic incidents every time I slip on a robe.

JIM: In the amazing account of your life, we keep reading this little phrase that indicates "God was with you." What do these words mean to you?

JOE: Seems I always knew God was with me. I never had a sense that he ever left me at any time or in any circumstances.

JIM: That's a wonderful feeling to have, but how do you get it? What's the basis for it?

JOE: Well, since it all happened, I've gone back and analyzed pretty thoroughly what Moses wrote about my experiences. All my responses were based on a growing knowledge of who God is. Without that, I'd have gone under more than once. If God was with me in Canaan and revealed himself to me, he was personal. If he was with me in Egypt, he was not just a local god; he was omnipresent. When he was with me as a slave and prisoner, he was merciful, loving, and faithful.

JIM: For most of us, it's easy to say nice things about God when things are going well. We say, "I didn't get a pink slip in that layoff. Ah, God is good." But you were stressed out with some really bad times, and you still said it.

JOE: Well, if God is good, that means trials are for a purpose. A good God wouldn't bring difficulty into our lives without good reason. In my case, I believe he wanted me to know what kind of a man I was: Could I still bring glory to him even in times of acute stress?

JIM: Now that's something I wanted to comment on. It appears to me that your associates were also very aware that God was with you. Is this true?

JOE: Yes. Others saw my success, but they knew it was God working through me.

JIM: Why would godless people think that?

JOE: Because I told them that God, not I, was doing it.

JIM: And that convinced Potiphar and the jailer and Pharaoh?

JOE: Well, perhaps my consistent trust in God, regardless of the circumstances, had something to do with it, too.

JIM: That's another important factor, isn't it? You learned to trust in this God regardless of what happened.

JOE: Why wouldn't I? God always came through. He always did what he said he would, sometimes in the most surprising ways. That's what I chose to remember, his faithfulness. You know, I named my first child Manasseh. It's a kind of a pun. Manasseh sounds something like our word for *forget*. God gave me a good life in Egypt and made me forget all those stressful times.

JIM: God is specifically mentioned more than eighty times in the story of your life. Your relationship to him was obviously very important. Could you summarize what you learned through those years of walking with him?

JOE: I can boil the whole thing down into five principles:

1. God is omnipresent. He is always with us in both good and bad circumstances.

2. God is omniscient. He is always aware of what is happening to us.

3. He is omnipotent. He can radically change our cir-

cumstances any time he wants.

4. God is worthy of trust. If my response under pressure is correct, others will see the reality of God reflected in my life.

5. God is unchangeable. He will even use evil over which I have no control to good purpose in my life.

JIM: I think the last of your principles is the one that impresses me most. Just those few words you spoke to your brothers—when they came to Egypt looking for food and you finally admitted your identity—tell us an awful lot about you. The words recorded in Genesis 50:20 ...

JOE: I still remember what I said to them: "You intended to harm me, but God intended it for good to accomplish what is now being done, the saving of many lives." It was true then, and it's true now.

Remember stressed-out Eddie at the beginning of this chapter? Sitting there considering suicide, he could not clearly identify any of these life-saving principles that Joseph understood. But at least he knew he wanted God to be present in his life. Instead of pulling the trigger, he took the first of several simple steps that helped him regain emotional and spiritual balance. He began to discover that God was, in fact, with him even in the midst of wrenching life changes, and he began to grow.

The Second Mile

1. Restudy Joseph's life. Draw a graph that shows his ups and downs as a teenager (Gn 37); an alien (Gn 39:1-19); and a prisoner (Gn 39:20-41:40).

2. As we've discussed, the text of Joseph's story repeats the phrase "God was with him." What does this mean? What would it mean if someone said it about you?

3. Can you give some specific reasons why God was able to use stress in Joseph's life as a tool for growth?

4. Is God with you in the sense that he was with Joseph? To rephrase the question: Is your heart attuned to God and his Word and his ways? Take this three-minute test and see where you stand. Rate yourself from one to five for each answer (five is high; one is low).

   a. Others prosper in their relationship with me (Gn 39:5).

   b. I acknowledge sexual immorality as sin and resist it (Gn 39:9).

   c. When things are tough, I know God has not abandoned me (Gn 39:21).

   d. I constantly acknowledge God in my daily affairs (various references).

   e. I recognize my own limitations and allow God to work through me (Gn 40:8, 16).

   f. I trust God to do what he says (Gn 40:21-22).

   g. I see myself as God's servant (Gn 41:15-16).

   h. I know suffering has a purpose (Gn 41:52).

   i. I recognize God as the reason for any success I have (Gn 45:5, 7-8).

   j. I believe God can use evil for good (Gn 50:20).

Total your answers and multiply by two.

94–100: Gracefully accept your "coat of many colors" medal.

85–93: You are growing through the stresses in your life.

75–84: You're coming along, but could have been better prepared for the test. (Review question e and ask God to continue his work.)

50–74: Maybe you should steer clear of your boss's spouse.

5. On which of the ten items in the test above do you most need to work? How will you do this? Specify appropriate action for each item.

love Jericho style

Rahab: The Single Who Gave Up on Promiscuity

For Rahab's story, see Joshua 2:1-21; 6:22-25.

I remember vividly my last visit to a house of prostitution. It was in dusty Imperatriz, a river town in northeastern Brazil that burst into life when President Jucelino Kubechek decided to slash a two-lane road through the green jungle between Brasilia and Belém to the north. A deacon and I representing the local church were making house-to-house visits that hot Sunday afternoon, hoping to sell some Bibles or Scripture portions and witness where we could. As we walked through a sparsely populated part of town, Manuel pointed to the next house up ahead. "That's where the prostitute lives," he said matter-of-factly.

The house had nothing to distinguish it from any other we had visited, but I was not surprised. In most of the scores of towns where I'd led every-home colportage campaigns, there was a red-light district or at least a house of prostitution. We carefully followed the pattern established by Jesus in the Gospels. We went out two by two and, also like Jesus, didn't avoid reaching out to prostitutes.

The door was open (everyone's was in these steamy interior towns), and the deacon clapped his hands to announce our presence. The woman who came to the door looked like an ordinary, pleasingly plump, Brazilian housewife except that she was wearing an excessive amount of gold jewelry. She extended her hand and the deacon shook it. She turned to me. I took her hand, and she escorted us into a rather sparsely furnished living room. A solitary man lounged sullenly in one corner.

We introduced ourselves, showed our Scriptures, and briefly explained the gospel. She wasn't interested. We shook hands again and left. I don't know about the deacon, but I felt as if her touch had somehow befouled me. I had an intense desire to plunge my hand into a bucket of hot, soapy water and scrub away the moral filthiness of her handclasp.

I wonder. Did the two spies that Joshua sent to Jericho feel as I did when they took the hand of Rahab, the bejeweled, perfumed woman waiting for them at the top of the stairs in that house of ill repute (see Jos 2:1)? It seems they knew this was a "house" and not a home, and it seems they were going to make this their motel while they reconnoitered the city's defenses and military strength and gauged the morale of its population.

As espionage goes, the assignment given the Jericho spies was not terribly difficult. Unlike the twelve Israelite spies who had gone north from Kadish-barnea nearly forty years before, they didn't have to roam all over the country and carry back a heavy load of produce. Instead, here they were, 840 feet below sea level, comfortably ensconced in the most ancient inhabited city in Palestine we know anything about. After a long trek in the desert for these sojourners, the abundance of water and swaying green palm groves must have been a refreshing delight. And as for their abode: A brothel may have been the safest place for them to stay.

As it turned out though, they were almost immediately discovered. Apparently some of Rahab's clientele knew their way around the palace. Someone went straight to the king, perhaps after observing the two Israelites having supper at Rahab's table. Why would two nice Jewish boys be in a house of ill fame unless they were spies?

Rahab's Hideaway

Joshua 2 continues the story of Rahab. Fortunately for the two spies, Rahab was a practiced liar. When the king's well-armed messengers arrived, demanding that she produce the two visitors from the east bank of the Jordan, she set them up by telling the truth. "Two Israelites? My dear sirs, please understand that my guest list must be held in strictest confidence.... But, yes, I do believe I, er, entertained a couple of guests who fit your description."

Having established her credibility by reluctantly sharing confidential information, Rahab looked her inquisitors square in the eyes and told three outrageous lies: (1) They're gone. (2) They left the city; other than that I don't know where they went. (3) Hurry! You may overtake them.

Where were the men really? Joshua's two spies were on the roof of Rahab's house. Hardly daring to breathe, they wondered why this shameless woman was risking her neck to save their lives. Rahab herself had hidden them under stalks of flax spread to dry on her flat roof.

What was the powerful motivation that drove Rahab to take such a fancy to these two strangers? It must have been compelling in the extreme, for her traitorous act of concealing them from local authorities virtually guaranteed the downfall of Jericho.

Rahab's motivation was based on her very sound knowledge of history and theology. This woman's information about God and his people was astonishing. Let's continue with her story. It had grown dark. The coast seemed to be clear. The spies had not yet gone to sleep, when she climbed to the roof, ready to exercise her finely honed art of persuasion as if her life depended on it—because it did!

Rahab told the Israelite men what she had heard about their people and what she believed about their God. "I know that the Lord has given this land to you and that a great fear of you has fallen on us, so that all who live in this country are melting in fear because of you. We have heard …" (vv. 9-10). She then gave an account of recent happenings. If there had been a newspaper in Jericho, I expect you might have found a clipping something like this on Rahab's dressing table. She would have read and reread the report of the recent events until she knew it almost by heart:

Israelites Complete Amorite Occupation;
Large Force Moves West to Jordan River

Israelite troops are concluding mopping-up operations twenty miles to the east after decisive victories over King Sihon of Heshbon and King Og of Bashan. All Amorite settlements and cities formerly controlled by the two kings are under Israelite occupation.

Before he was beheaded, Sihon admitted a major tactical error in refusing the Israelite nomads safe passage up the King's Highway as they had requested.

A large group of Israelites are reported to be crossing the plains of Moab. They appear to be headed to an encampment on the east side of the Jordan just eight miles from Jericho.

Authorities report that city gates are now closed to all but emergency traffic, and every precaution is being taken to secure the city against a surprise attack or any Israelite attempts of espionage.

Yes, Rahab knew about Israel's future: This land will belong to the Israelites. She knew about the past too, including the miraculous Red Sea crossing when Israel had fled from Egyptian slavery. She certainly knew about the present. An invasion was imminent and Jericho would have the questionable honor of being the first Canaanite city to be conquered. In all of this—past, present, and future—she knew that the hand of the Israelite God, Jehovah, was powerfully at work.

What Rahab Knew About God

The fact that everyone in Canaan was expecting an invasion doesn't surprise me too much. What does make me wonder is the extent of Rahab's knowledge about the Israelite God. Read and note the wording of Joshua 2:8-13. She probably knew quite a bit more than some of our average pew warmers today. The names she used for God are highly significant. She called him "the Lord" six times. This was the Jewish national name for God, the Hebrew word *YHWH* or *Yahweh*. Most Bibles translate it as "Lord," because in late Old Testament times Jews regarded *Yahweh* as too holy to pronounce, substituting the word *Adonai (Jehovah)* or *Lord*. *Yahweh* means "the self-existent or eternal one." It's the descriptive verb God himself used when he spoke to Moses at the burning bush. "I am who I am" or "I will be who I will be."

When she talked to the spies about "your God," Rahab used the Hebrew word *Elohim*. This was *El*, the generic word for god (as in *El*, the father of the principal Canaanite god Baal). But here Rahab used its plural form, which would be the equivalent of a superlative and turn the meaning into "the supreme God." Both terms appear in Deuteronomy 5:9. "I, the Lord [Jehovah] your God [Elohim], am a jealous God [El]."

Now before you become overly impressed with all this God-talk, remember who's talking. Wouldn't you be just a little skeptical of what a prostitute had to say about God? Perhaps, but what Rahab said next takes us beyond just "talking a good talk" to personal belief. She says, "The Lord your God is God in heaven above and on the earth below" (v. 11). Translation: Jehovah, the Supreme Being you Israelites recognize, is above and independent of the material universe, and yet he's here on earth too.

Taken all together Rahab's theology seems pretty impressive, especially in view of her limited resources. She recognized Jehovah as the sovereign Lord of Lords who intervenes in human history. He is almighty and his purposes cannot be thwarted. If J.I. Packer had been around, I think Rahab would certainly have agreed with what he wrote in his book *Knowing God:* "What He does in time, He planned from eternity. And all that He planned in eternity He carries out in time. And all that He has in His word committed Himself to do will infallibly be done."

Rahab's astonishing acceptance of this revolutionary idea of God is hard for us to gauge in a culture 3,400 years removed from hers. In his book *Heritage: Civilization and the Jews,* statesman-scholar Abba Eban helps us tune in to the ancient polytheistic culture that pervaded the Middle East in Rahab's time:

Even the smallest Canaanite city-states seemed to have a more developed material culture than the Jews. But the Jews did have a startling revolutionary idea, the idea of a single God presiding over the course of nature and the fate of mankind, with Himself independent of them both.

We can understand how revolutionary this idea was if we compare it with Egyptian, Mesopotamian, and Canaanite environments. The monuments of these cultures include gods with human heads and animal bodies, bulls with wings, birds with four legs. To equate divinity with beasts is to degrade mankind below the human level. Clearly, those civilizations, with all their outward sophistication and refinement, were plunged in a deep confusion of spirit. Magical and orgiastic rites flowed naturally from such an inharmonious vision of nature.

The Jewish vision of God was totally out of tune with the ideas of the pagan world. One God, invisible, supreme, without life or death, without passion or lust. From this there came an idea of unity and order. Man had a power of choice: Progress, not repetition, was the law of life. Man was not the helpless victim of a natural cycle.

Rahab had obviously grasped a large and significant hunk of truth. How would she react to it? In several different ways we are told that she was terrified—along with all the citizens of Jericho.

The other morning at breakfast a friend laughed as he told me how his family reacted to "War of the Worlds." The 1938 hour-long Orson Welles radio drama was interrupted by what purported to be the eyewitness account of a Martian invasion. Although there were two disclaimers during the program, millions of listeners, like my friend and his family, panicked when they were told hideous creatures from outer space had invaded New Jersey. My friend learned the truth only when his father arrived home from work. The family went to bed without fear because they felt assured that no aliens would be landing in Minnesota that night. How different this situation from that of Rahab and the citizens of Jericho!

Fear of Death, Hope of Life

For Rahab, nothing could have been more believable than the impending invasion. Her response, based on fact, was motivated by fear. She negotiated an agreement with the two spies. It's almost legal in its length, language, and completeness, but here's what it boils down to: Safe passage of the spies out of the city was to guarantee safe passage for Rahab and her family when (not if!) Jericho was invaded and conquered by the Israelites.

There's no way Rahab could have foreseen the full significance of this agreement. The most immediate benefit was certainly encouraging. She and her family would not be among the bloody corpses lying in the streets when Israelite warriors torched the city. But what about her profession? What would become of her? Where would she live? How would she live?

Rahab, could we take time out here for a little chat? Yes, I know you're pretty nervous. Everything depends on those spies making it safely back across the river. But just listen to me for a minute. With all the changes that are about to take place in your life, don't you think this would be a good time to include your promiscuous lifestyle? You've clearly said you want to be on the winning side, God's side. Do you think there's any way this God in heaven above and on the earth below is going to be pleased with the way you've been living?

Over the years singles have confided in me their struggles with sex outside of marriage. Rob, a young, recently divorced truck driver, was surprised by God's power in this area of his life: "I thought this was going to be an impossible situation for me," he said, "but God is helping me handle it." For others, it's a question of spiritual growth. Another man with an attractive female friend told me the other day, "We're not fooling around. I don't believe in that anymore."

God's Plan for Sex

If the motivation for these two men is commitment to biblical principles and spiritual growth, for many others the motivation is fear. God's plan for sex only within the context of marriage is clear in the Scriptures, but for some singles biblical prohibition doesn't speak strongly enough. And yet now, with the widespread risk of sexually transmitted disease among heterosexuals, even singles without religious convictions have decided to stop or at least limit their casual sexual encounters.

Even so, to many the words *chastity* and *abstinence* conjure up an abnormal, repulsive, unimaginably Victorian lifestyle. Researching for her book *Purity Makes the Heart Grow Stronger*, Julia Duin found she could not even use these terms if she wanted to get valid results. One friend of mine confirmed this current mind-set. Sex is often the topic around the table during his coffee break at the office. He is definitely a minority of one in his biblical view of sex. His colleagues can't believe anyone today would not see the advantage of bedding any willing partner.

I would encourage any contemporary Christian single to take the difficult and unpopular choice of abstinence. I particularly like Eugene H. Peterson's paraphrase of 1 Peter 1:13-16: "Don't lazily slip back into those old grooves of evil, doing just what you feel like doing. You didn't know any better then; you do now. As obedient children, let yourselves be pulled into a way of life shaped by God's life, a life energetic and blazing with holiness. God said, 'I am holy; you be holy'" (THE MESSAGE).

The Rest of the Story

Rahab must have assimilated some of these ideas in their Old Testament form. I say this because we have just a little glimpse of what happened to her after Jericho was conquered. But let's not get ahead of our story. One of Rahab's agreements with the spies was that she would positively identify her house, which was a part of or "on" the city wall. As per their agreement, she did this by tying a red cord in the window through which she helped the spies escape.

How long do you think it took her to do that? I think it was right after the spies escaped. She pulled in the swaying rope dangling down the side of the city wall, hid it in a chest, and looked over at her bed. I imagine there was a red cord on the canopy. "I don't think I'll be needing this anymore," she may have said to no one in particular. She pulled the cord down, tassels and all, and knotted it securely in the window.

As recorded in Joshua 5–6, Joshua's strategy for conquering Jericho was unconventional to say the least. March the army around the city for seven days, God instructed, with seven priests blowing rams' horns. No one was supposed to talk, but I imagine the first time around the city, the two spies silently searched for that window with a red cord. One looked up, saw it, and gave a thumbs up: "There it is! That's Rahab's house."

When the walls fell on the seventh day, the Israelite army invaded the city. Every living thing was put to death, except for a frightened little family huddled in that house in the "red-rope district." I wonder: Had Rahab's family ever been there before, and how did they feel about visiting her place of business? They heard shouts, then someone running up the stairs. Pounding on the securely barred door. Was it the spies or had the king's soldiers gotten there ahead of them? Rahab looked out the peephole. The two spies themselves had climbed the stairs and were there to escort her, her parents, brothers, and their servants outside the city to safety.

The story has an even happier ending when we pick up the final facts about Rahab. Joshua 6:25 notes that Rahab "lives among the Israelites to this day." But maybe that's not the whole story. Rahab is mentioned three times in the New Testament. Would you be surprised to find her included in Matthew's genealogy of Christ? She married a man named Salmon. She and this very forgiving man had a son named Boaz who married a foreigner named Ruth. They had a son named Obed who fathered Jesse, the father of King David. You get the picture. Rahab was King David's great, great grandmother and an ancestor of the Messiah.

So Rahab did clean up her life of promiscuity. Like many singles I know, she decided the best way to do this was to get married. The apostle Paul, in his classic treatment of the subject in 1 Corinthians 7, commends marriage. "If they cannot control themselves, they should marry, for it is better to marry than to burn with passion" (v. 9). For others who have the gift of singleness, every single day is a challenge to remain pure.

Was Rahab's Conversion Real?

I have a keen interest in what I might call Rahab's conversion experience. Did she really have the kind of personal faith that brought her into a right relationship with God? James and the writer of Hebrews both give us a resounding yes. She was not just a calculating, opportunistic risk taker, looking out for number one, as some of her friends may have thought. She was a woman who believed and acted on her belief. James 2:25 says,

"Was not even Rahab the prostitute considered righteous for what she did when she gave lodging to the spies and sent them off in a different direction?"

In Hebrews 11 Rahab is listed in the company of Noah, Abraham, Moses, and a great company of men and women of faith. The pattern is clear. She knew the truth, believed it, and acted upon it in faith. Maybe you're asking this question, as proffered by Gien Karssen in *Her Name Is Woman (Book 1):* "Rahab ... a heroine of faith? Yes. For God is no respecter of persons. There are no impossible cases with Him. He justifies the ungodly."

Some readers may feel their sexual past in some way marks them, as if their sin were too great for Christ to forgive. In that regard, I consider this story related by Elisabeth Elliot in her book *Passion and Purity.*

My friend Calvin Thielman ... tells the story of an old Scottish preacher who, as he was serving the bread and wine of the Lord's Supper noticed a young girl sobbing at the communion rail. As he passed her the bread, visible sign of the body of the Lord Jesus ("I give it for the life of the world," He said) the girl turned away her face, which was wet with tears.

"Tak' it, lassie," said the old man. "It's for sinners."

This week, as I knelt in prayer before my God, tears ran down my cheeks too. I thanked him for showing me for the first time hidden sins in my life that I'd never seen before. He's known all along of course, and that's why before the foundation of the world he provided forgiveness "in accordance with the riches of [his] grace that he lavished on us with all wisdom and understanding" (Eph 1:7-8).

A House Becomes a Home

Can God infiltrate a house of prostitution? Obviously, he can. Once this happens there's going to be a difference. There's a difference because his indwelling presence is going to shine out through actions, reactions, attitudes, and conversations and communicate a new value system in a house that becomes a home. On the other hand, if our commitment to God's presence is superficial, people will see an inconsequential God who demands little respect or attention.

How do you relate to the sexual byplay that goes on in many workplaces? If you want to reflect God's view of sex, you will have to let people know you do not wish to participate. If that doesn't work, would you be willing to quit your job and look for something else? Rahab didn't just quit her job; she risked her life to get out of the situation she was in.

On a more personal level, how do you react to opportunities for sexual intimacy outside of marriage? One young widow I know was wise. She knew the answer to this question before she went out on a dinner date with a promising professional. During the meal he kept making what he thought were complimentary remarks about her body. As they stood to leave the restaurant, he offered one final observation that went over the line. "I'm not sleeping with you tonight or any other night," she said bluntly. He hasn't called since, and she's glad. If sex has to be the basis of a relationship before marriage, she isn't interested. Whether or not she ever marries again, she knows obedience brings its own rewards. Check out Psalm 81:13a, 16:

If my people would but listen to me....
You would be fed with the finest of wheat;
with honey from the rock I would satisfy you.

Maybe you've fallen in love with someone, and you aren't sure that love can wait until the wedding. Consider this comment by D.G. Kehl, author of *Control Yourself: Practicing the Art of Self-Discipline:*

Self-discipline requires us to do what comes supernaturally. How can we learn to master our bodies in holiness and honor rather than in the gratification of our passions? Paul gives the secret in [1 Thessalonians 4]: because it is His will that we be holy (v. 3), God has *called* us into holiness (v. 7), and has given us His Spirit, who is holy (v. 8). Mastery of the body must come from the *inside out,* through the Spirit's control, rather than from the *outside in,* through a program or regimen.

Genuine self-discipline of the body is essentially mind over matter—the mind of Christ over the matter of our bodies.

I think of an old hymn-prayer by John Greenleaf Whittier that might give you strength to resist sexual temptation.

Breathe through the heats of our desire
Thy coolness and thy balm;
Let sense be dumb, let flesh retire;

Speak through the earthquake, wind, and fire,
O still, small voice of calm.

Here are a few things I've learned from Rahab and from the years I've spent ministering among singles:

1. Your actions, reactions, and conversations with the opposite sex clearly reveal what you believe about God.

2. If your God is real, intimate, personal, and powerful, like the God of Rahab, your relationship with the opposite sex will reflect these ideas in your behavior.

3. If your relationship with God is superficial, a mere convenience, a sometime friendship, your life is likely to be troubled with casual sex.

4. The knowledge of God that changed Rahab's life can change your life too, especially if you're having difficulty accepting God's guidelines for sex.

Thanks, Rahab, for having the kind of theology that is worth not only believing in, but acting on and living out. Now, if you don't mind, I'd like to bother you with just one more question: Was Salmon, your Prince Charming, one of the spies?

The Second Mile

1. Do you think Rahab's story might be a good case history for someone who says he or she is too great a sinner to become a Christian? What line of argument would you use?

2. Hebrews 11:31 says Rahab's life was spared because she was not among "those who were disobedient." What does this mean?

3. Here are some attributes of God. Choose an appropriate, specific response to each. A couple of answers are given to get you started.

Majestic: *Worship*

Giver:

Unchangeable: *Consistent lifestyle*

Wise:

Faithful:

Redeemer:

4. Consider these additional qualities that describe a perfect, eternal, unchangeable God: holy, loving, merciful, truthful, good, patient, just. Which one does your life reflect with the least distortion? Which one needs the most work?

5. Is there some biblical truth you know very well but are reluctant to respond to because of the cost? Use the form below to evaluate your situation, then make a decision based on what you discover.

Stay Where I Am		Do What I Know I Ought to Do	
Gain	Loss	Gain	Loss

what if God came to your pity party?

Elijah: The Single Who Was Depressed

For the story of Elijah, see 1 Kings 17–19.

Her teenaged sons found out before she did. "Mom," the oldest began reluctantly one afternoon, "we don't know how to tell you this." It was obviously bad news.

"Then just tell me," Mary snapped.

"Ann's already moved in with Dad."

It's just too classic, Mary thought. *But didn't I guess it was his secretary?*

Of course, even before her husband left the note on her dressing table and disappeared, Mary knew something was wrong. Their quarrels had intensified over the last year or two. She still had her striking good looks, but nothing—flowers, perfume, slinky nightgowns—got any response in the bedroom. Then her husband stopped saying he loved her, looked faintly embarrassed when she kissed him. Said it was just a phase he was going through. But it wasn't a phase. The gulf between them widened.

Mary called her husband—the call arranged by her pastor.

After they talked, she hung up and a numbness invaded her whole being. "This is what I want," the voice on the other end had said. "I'm not coming back." It was final, then. God was not going to answer her prayers. She slept from sheer exhaustion but didn't awaken rested. Did she eat breakfast? Did she eat lunch? By the time a close friend came over, Mary wasn't sure. But finally she was able to cry. After that she couldn't stop. The most unexpected, insignificant things would start a Niagara of tears.

Mary kept going to work, but she couldn't concentrate. It didn't take a rocket scientist to see she wasn't getting her work done. Her understanding boss saw the problem and offered her a week off. She took it. At home the boys soon learned it didn't take much to set her off. They stayed pretty much to their rooms. She was glad, because she didn't want anyone around at all.

To each other the boys talked about their mom. They were too young to understand the overwhelming guilt she felt or the loss of self-worth that went with it. She felt she had failed in the most important task God had given her. She turned over and over in her mind a million things she could have done differently. She felt so alone; the aloneness that enveloped Mary brought an ache so deep and so intense she didn't know how she could stand it another day.

Then one evening at the mall she saw her husband and "the other woman." He leaned across a table in the food court and kissed her tenderly. When Mary got home she opened the medicine cabinet and stared at a bottle of pills. The past was past; the present was a disaster. There was nothing she could see in her future that could possibly make life worth living. It was a long time before she shut the cabinet door and stumbled off to bed.

Classic Symptoms

Mary didn't know it yet, but the emotions she was experiencing are classic symptoms of severe depression. She didn't realize she was depressed even when it became painfully obvious that her friends were avoiding her. You see, Mary had become quite contrary. And everywhere that Mary went, you could spot little black clouds all in a row.

Elijah the prophet may have been a lot like that. Everywhere he went, it seemed, he brought bad news. A cloud of doom descended, and people around him became depressed. Jewish novelist Isaac Bashevis Singer described Elijah pretty well during an interview on *The Dick Cavett Show:* "If you keep saying things are going to be bad, you have a chance of being a prophet."

A Price on His Head

Well, Elijah *was* a prophet and he did say things were going to be bad. As his story begins, in 1 Kings 17, Elijah went to Jezreel, the summer capital of Israel, with a prophetic word for the evil King Ahab: Drought and famine were on the way. The people of Samaria were in for unimaginable suffering, financial ruin, and even death.

Having delivered the word, Elijah wisely followed the Lord's leading, hurried into exile, and camped by a stream. God miraculously provided meat and bread every day and Elijah drank from the stream. But after a while it seemed that even the stream wanted to get rid of this gloomy man. The stream dried up, and Elijah began a long trek northward.

He invited himself into the home of a desperately poor widow. He hoped he could help her and at the same time become invisible to angry King Ahab, who had put a price on his head.

Once again, for "some time" God miraculously provided food for Elijah, the widow, and her family. But one day the widow's son got sick and stopped breathing. The widow blamed Elijah. "What do you have against me, man of God? Did you come to remind me of my sin and kill my son?" (1 Kgs 17:18).

Pleading with God, Elijah revived the boy. Elijah stayed there longer, but eventually, at God's direction, traveled south toward Jezreel and met his fellow prophet, Obadiah, who, fearing for his own life, arranged a meeting between Elijah and King Ahab. When Ahab saw Elijah waiting on the far side of a field, he called bitterly, "Is that you, you troubler of Israel?" (1 Kgs 18:17).

Elijah arranged a test between Ahab's god, Baal, and the Lord God. On Mount Carmel, Baal proved silent, powerless. God, on the other hand, sent fire down to consume the sacrifice on the altar. Elijah directed the Israelites to kill the 450 prophets of Baal, and, yes, it started to rain. The three-and-a-half-year drought ended as a torrential rain pounded the countryside.

Elijah then raced down the mountain and ran all the way to Jezreel. Far into the night Elijah waited for news. At best, he

hoped to hear of Ahab's decision to abolish idolatry and insti-
tute the worship of the true God, Jehovah. He at least hoped
for a royal commendation for ending the drought. But a messenger from the queen appeared. "Jezebel says to tell you
you're dead meat. Before sundown tomorrow, she'll have
you!" the runner sneered.

Elijah again ran for his life—this time he headed south, into
Judah, wishing himself dead. Should we be surprised that
someone whose presence invariably meant bad news and
depression for those around him had a problem with depression himself? A few days after God's absolutely stunning
demonstration of his power and presence, we hear an exhausted, clinically depressed Elijah voicing thoughts of suicide.
"I have had enough, Lord. Take my life; I am no better than
my ancestors" (1 Kgs 19:4).

A Common Complaint

If your problem is feeling sorry for yourself, you're not alone.
Abraham Lincoln frequently dreamed of seeing his own coffin.
Vincent van Gogh cut off his ear during a fit of despair just
before Christmas 1888. Winston Churchill called depression
the "black dog." It shadowed him through life and finally
immobilized him during his last years. Contemporary figures
like actress Patty Duke and newsman Mike Wallace have experienced serious bouts with depression.

Pastors and other Christian workers are not immune. Joni
Eareckson Tada, Ben Patterson, and Florence Littauer have
written of their bouts with depression. (See their accounts in

Dark Clouds, Silver Linings by Archibald Hart.) John Calvin, Martin Luther, John Wesley, and Charles Spurgeon were well acquainted with the malady. And if you want examples of depression from the Bible, the list is almost endless: Cain (see Gn 4:13-14); Abraham (see Gn 17:18); Jacob at Joseph's purported death (see Gn 37); Saul (see 1 Sm 16:14-23); Ahithophel (see 2 Sm 17:23); Job; David (dip into the Psalms); Jeremiah (see Jer 20:7-18); and even Jesus. As the horror of his betrayal and crucifixion neared, the Man of Sorrows told his friends, "My soul is overwhelmed with sorrow to the point of death" (Mk 14:34).

Depression seems to be endemic in contemporary America. In fact it's our leading form of mental illness and is a health problem ranked as serious as diabetes and leukemia. *Newsweek* once reported that of all the suicides in the United States each year, as many as half occur among people suffering from depression. Suicide needn't be the solution. The prospects for recovery are bright, as we shall see.

"Elijah was a man just like us," James 5:17 tells us. "He prayed earnestly that it would not rain, and it did not rain on the land for three and a half years." James is saying that ordinary people like you and me can get extraordinary answers to prayer. The fact that Elijah experienced severe depression only serves to underscore his humanity.

So let's look at this "ordinary" man and see if we can learn something about depression. What is it? Where does it come from? How do you get rid of it?

The severe depression that Elijah experienced was brought on by a series of significant losses. For Elijah and for us, these losses bring stress, grieving, and depression. We don't get the expected promotion. We move and lose familiar surroundings. A dear friend moves away. An act of bravery fails to pay off. The guy doesn't get the girl or vice versa. We look in the mirror, and it tells us we are getting older. We disappoint God in some way, and he seems very far away.

If any of this sounds familiar, you can join Elijah's club, for these are the very things he experienced. They brought on a crushing downer that pushed him to the brink of suicide. Because of what had happened in the past and the present, he could see no hope for the future. What did he feel? In her article "Beating Depression" in *U.S. News and World Report* (March 5, 1990), reporter Erica Good gleaned some interesting descriptives. One depressed man said it's like being in quicksand. "There's a sense of doom, of sadness." Another called depression "a veritable howling tempest in the brain."

Symptoms of Severe Depression

I think Elijah would say a fervent amen to those descriptions, and for good reason. He had all the classic symptoms of severe depression.

1. Loss of Hope
Let's pick up Elijah's story when he's standing at the entrance of Jezreel (see 1 Kgs 18:46, KJV). It must have been after midnight, his clothes were soaked, and he was exhausted from the events of an emotion-charged day. Exhilarated by the pouring rain that had followed his mountaintop prayer, he had made a

twenty-three-mile, adrenaline-fed run down Mount Carmel.

What was he doing as he rested there by the gate? We can't know, but I think he was praying. Praying that the seventh in a string of evil kings was going to stand Israel on its head with a sweeping reformation. "O Lord, King Ahab saw what happened on the mountain today. Help him convince his Baal-worshiping wife, Jezebel, that Jehovah is the true God. Cause them both to turn to you, Lord. Let her lead in restoring our places of worship. Use this powerful military leader and his wife for your glory! Guide them to bring about the national revival you've been using me to push them toward for three and a half years now."

If this was Elijah's prayer, it wasn't to be answered. Jezebel's messenger found him there. Elijah didn't "get the girl," and God didn't either. In fact, she was out to get him. The public ministry Elijah had hardly begun was ended. He was an exile again with a price on his head. Despair and sadness seeped through his weary body. His outlook was as dark and foreboding as the shadowed streets of Jezreel.

2. Loss of Self-Esteem

By this time Elijah's self-confidence was just about nonexistent. What was a prophet supposed to do? He'd heard God's voice, announced the message to the people, and waited for them to turn to God. Some did, but he had expected the nation as a whole to turn to the worship of Jehovah. Maybe he'd hoped to be the new prime minister or the nation's spiritual guide. Not so. No one will ever have a more powerful altar call than they had on that mountaintop overlooking the Mediterranean, but sweeping revival did not come. And Elijah perceived himself a failure. He'd failed God. He'd failed the nation. He'd failed in his vocation.

3. Difficulty Handling Emotions

I think Elijah was struggling with fear, despair, and especially anger. A few days ago he'd been fearlessly giving the king orders. Now the queen had vowed to kill him. Would he have to hide out again in the attic at that crotchety widow's house? He was feeling a sense of complete worthlessness. And he was in a total rage. Ahab had betrayed him. How could Jezebel possibly misunderstand the massacre of her 450 priests? "Doesn't she know I did the right thing? God, even you let me down. Yes, the people said, 'Jehovah—he is God!' but it'll never stick." Elijah could see dawn was still several hours off. *There's only one thing to do,* he thought. He tucked his cloak into his belt again and started running as hard as he could.

4. Desire to Escape Problems

Remember when you were little and thought your parents were being unreasonable? You announced defiantly that you were running away from home and went to your room to pack. You desperately wanted to get away, put distance between you and your problem; escape the circumstances that had conspired so unjustly against you.

That's exactly what Elijah did. Running away from Jezreel may not have been a bad idea for Elijah, but this desire to escape can be a symptom of depression. Twice in 1 Kings 17, the writer says that God told Elijah to flee—get out of danger. But this later passage simply says that Elijah "was afraid and ran for his life" (1 Kgs 19:3). He headed south.

5. Loss of Perspective

The mounting number of losses that Elijah suffered, both real and imagined, seriously distorted his way of perceiving things. For more than three years he had found a secure haven in the widow's home in Zeraphath. But in this crisis, under the cover of darkness, Elijah had sped south, Zeraphath getting farther away by the minute.

Professionally, Elijah felt he was ruined, his career over. He had pulled out all the stops there on the mountain and what had he gotten? A royal appointment? Freedom to come and go announcing God's messages? I think that in his depressed state Elijah had what Joni Eareckson Tada calls "the quiet rage"; it had so twisted his thinking process that he could neither recognize nor accept success. In other words, he wasn't seeing his circumstances at all as God saw them. God had brought spectacular victory for Elijah in the mountaintop contest between himself and Baal. True, the nation and its leadership had not lived up to Elijah's expectations. But their response wasn't his responsibility, was it? Elijah was the kind of person Winston Churchill described as "snatching defeat from the jaws of victory." That's what depression does to us.

Elijah's perspective had become totally self-centered. He was convinced he was a failure, a fugitive, a man without a future. Hope? He had none.

He was about to settle down under a tree in the middle of nowhere and start his pity party in earnest. If you've lost some of the key elements that orient your life, including career, spouse, home, hobby, anything else dear to you, you know the feeling.

6. Change in Eating and Sleeping Habits

Some people who experience depression go on an eating binge. Some virtually stop eating. It seems Elijah did the latter. He was a man in a fear-driven hurry; here was a man who needed to grab a Coke and fries at a fast-food drive-up window. There wasn't any window of course, so the prophet and his servant had to stop for food in some of the towns and villages on their flight path. But Elijah wouldn't linger. He forgot about three squares; he ate because he had to.

As for sleeping, there were big changes here too. I suspect the two men traveled by night and found a hiding place to sleep during the day. The image of an enraged Queen Jezebel kept their sleep times short and their travel time long. Elijah was losing pounds, losing sleep, and nearing total exhaustion.

7. Withdrawal From Others

Elijah was a long way from familiar surroundings when he got to Beersheba, a town in which he'd never been before. Everything seemed strange; he didn't know anyone there. Anonymity was just what this miserably unhappy man wanted. But his misery was not yet complete. He dismissed the servant who had faithfully run by his side for a week. I think Elijah may have been sick of this man's efforts to cheer him up. He didn't want to cheer up! Elijah then headed out into the desert another twelve miles or so. Misery *doesn't* love company.

Check it out. Significant loss can be real or imagined, but the result is the same. We withdraw. We cancel our favorite activities. Recorded messages fill the tape on our answering machine; we don't call back. We give lame excuses when someone invites us to a social event we normally would have accepted with pleasure.

8. Guilt

Try to think the way Elijah was thinking. His guilt was partly imagined, partly real, but either way it was tearing at his heart. I imagine he thought he'd let God down because revival hadn't come. He was certain he'd failed his people, as their national security depended upon their relationship with God. And he had failed as a man of God, hadn't he? After all, he had run when he should have stood his ground, even if it resulted in the death of one more prophet. Whether his evaluations were true or false, all were based on unrealistic expectations. Such a mixture cannot make a positive contribution to anyone's mental health.

9. Suicidal Thoughts

Elijah was totally alone now in the wilderness and his servant was a day's journey behind him. He may have thought of going farther (I believe his final destination lay another three hundred miles to the southeast), but he didn't have the will or strength to take one more step. He'd finally come to the end of himself. He sat down under the meager shade of a common bush. He prayed, "I have had enough, Lord. Take my life" (1 Kgs 19:4). He cryptically continued, in effect saying, *I'm as good as dead.*

Why did Elijah want to die? Check his dipstick physically, spiritually, emotionally. He was about five quarts low in every category. His life had been lived under incredible tension ever since he had boldly met King Ahab in the field outside Jezreel. He hadn't eaten properly or slept much for a long time. Since the fire came down on the mountain, he'd burned up more adrenaline than most men use in a lifetime. He was physically exhausted.

Spiritually Elijah had hit bottom too. The hope we all have to have to keep on living was gone. He saw no further use for himself or his ministry. He believed God was finished with him. His pessimism about the future was absolute. Everything worth living for was gone, so he figured he might as well die.

Scripture says Elijah then dropped off to sleep. Elijah's symptoms were typical of one of the more severe levels of depression. The manifestations of depression are incredibly complex. Intensities stretch across a broad range. Depression can be nothing more than the brooding funks we all experience when life throws us a curve. A leisurely hot bath or a friendly word of encouragement may bring us back to reality. On the other end of the spectrum are severe manifestations of depression where drugs, psychotherapy, or even hospitalization may be prescribed.

Elijah was in pretty bad shape, but the nearest psychiatric hospital would be a few millennia away. How would he find healing?

Healing Begins

Healing started for Elijah there under the broom tree when he opened up and honestly expressed his feelings to God. God was ready now to help him put an end to this pity party, and God knew just how to do it. After he'd slept awhile Elijah felt a hand gently rubbing across his shoulder. In scriptural accounts of angelic visits, usually the first phrase is "Don't be afraid," but this angel knew Elijah was too dead emotionally to react even to the supernatural presence. "Get up and eat," God's messenger said.

There's no record of a conversation. Just the gentle touch of someone who cared. A hot, fragrant loaf of bread was right there beside Elijah's head where he couldn't help but smell it. And there was a jar of water for his parched throat. God knew that, until serious physical problems were taken care of, there wasn't much that could be done about the spiritual or emotional.

Medical people today know that glands, muscles, blood vessels, and body chemicals play integral roles when it comes to depression—its cause or effects. Physically Elijah was a mess, in need of serious replenishment. Elijah ate the hot bread, drank some water, and fell asleep again. The angelic alarm clock went off again. Another gentle touch indicated it was time for another catered meal. God knew Elijah's trip had only begun and he needed strength for the trek before him. He was about to leave the rude shelter of his desert bush and travel south another three hundred miles, heading for a place on the Sinai Peninsula that would prove more beneficial than the couch of any twentieth-century psychotherapist.

The Mountain of God

In the Bible Elijah's destination is usually called Sinai, but the author of 1 Kings used the alternate name Horeb, "the Mountain of God." Its red and pink rocks push 7,500 feet above sea level on the southern end of the Sinai Peninsula.

From this holy, consecrated mountain, God had spoken to Moses, reaffirming the covenant with his people. From a mysterious thick cloud, he had spoken above the roar of an earthquake, of thunder, and of fire to give the Ten Commandments. Moses and Joshua had climbed this rugged mountain to receive the plans for the tabernacle. The Israelites waiting at the foot of the mountain had seen the glory of the Lord and it "looked like a consuming fire on top of the mountain" (Ex 24:17). *Elijah, are you sure this is where you want to go? Don't you remember that the children of Israel watched and trembled with fear? Don't you know that during the year when the people camped nearby, they were forbidden to go up the mountain on penalty of death?*

Perhaps the desperate prophet expected this new mountaintop experience to kill or cure him. Feeling some better, at least physically, he continued his journey of almost six weeks. He wasn't running now. He could have gotten there in half the time. He was beginning to regain a healthy, new perspective.

I think Elijah must have asked some important questions as he trudged down the desert trail. The toughest question: *What did I really lose, and what are the implications?* The next question may have been, *Can I accept my loss and allow myself to be sad, to grieve?* Accepting loss is an act of the will, and I'm not sure Elijah could do it yet. Later, on the mountain, he'd be able to put his loss in proper perspective as he saw it in relationship to the plan God had for his life.

It's interesting to compare Elijah's two mountaintop experiences. On Carmel he was a supercharged man of God bursting with confidence and courage. He was surrounded by shouting crowds and wailing prophets. The king was there.

But at the end of his desert walk (see 1 Kgs 19:9-14), he arrived at Sinai a few steps away from total despair. He was alone, except for the presence of the King of Kings, the God who never gives up. Natural phenomena played an important part in this encounter, just as they did for Moses. But first something happened that hadn't happened for a long time. God spoke to his prophet. "What are you doing here, Elijah?" (v. 9).

Did Elijah answer? Sort of. Elijah basically said, "Lord, we're pushing a lost cause here. It's all over. I'm here because I'm running for my life."

Had Elijah regained some of his perspective? How much of what he said was really true? Almost all of it. He had put his reputation, his career, and his very life on the line to bring his people from idolatry to the worship of the true God. It hadn't happened. There was once again a price on Elijah's head. But then Elijah made a complaint to God that wasn't based on reality: "I am the only one left" (v. 10), the only one who has remained faithful to God. Not true, Elijah.

God's Therapy

God wanted to bring his child out of the frustration of depression and back into a satisfying, full ministry. God wanted him to see his future with hope.

So let the therapy begin. God didn't accuse or condemn Elijah; he gently, quietly helped Elijah regain a true perspective of his life. God's first question to Elijah might be rephrased,

"Why are you here?" And the second: "Where do you think I am?" Considering those questions can start anyone on the road to mental health.

At God's request, Elijah stepped out of the cave in which he had spent the night. The God who had been so distant for so long was going to pass by. *This is a test, Elijah. Are you ready? Here comes a wind like you've never seen before.* A powerful, rock-shattering, mountain-tearing tornado passed by. "Did you see the Lord, Elijah?"

"Not yet."

"Brace yourself, Elijah. It's going to be a 7.5 on the Richter scale. Wow! It's over. I think. We can pick ourselves up now. Did you see the Lord, Elijah?"

"Not yet."

The last natural phenomenon was fire, presumably the same fire (lightning) that fell on Carmel. "Are you surprised, Elijah?" God wasn't even in the fire.

It must have been clear by now to Elijah that God was not going to answer the death wish of a deeply despondent man. He'd had three chances and yet hadn't even injured his servant there on that holy mountain. He intended to give life, not death. Elijah retreated to the safety of his cave at some point during the fearful meteorological display. It was quiet now. He heard a gentle whisper, pulled his cloak over his face, and advanced to the mouth of the cave.

God gently repeated his first question: "What are you doing here, Elijah?" It's as if God were saying, "Elijah, you didn't get it quite right the first time. I'm giving you another chance."

But Elijah didn't change a word of his answer. "I have been very zealous for the Lord God Almighty. The Israelites have rejected your covenant, broken down your altars, and put your prophets to death with the sword. I am the only one left, and now they are trying to kill me too" (v. 14).

Same question, same reply. Hidden in it are the three misperceptions of every depressed person: I am powerless, unworthy. My world is frustrating, my activities unfulfilling. My future is hopeless. In his book *Disordered Loves,* William Stafford gives a good, concise description of accidie, which I see as being equally descriptive of depression: "Accidie is partial consent to non-being, striking a bargain with insignificance." He also refers to it as a "bottomless dejection."

At this point God moved to help Elijah do what all of us must do if we want to escape our web of depression. We must move away from attachments to the person or thing we have lost and look forward to a new future. That's where hope lies and God knew it. He gave Elijah a new ministry and the assurance that he wasn't alone as he had thought. There were seven thousand Israelites who had never given their allegiance to Baal.

The assignment God gave Elijah was not just busywork. God would use him to change the history of Israel. "Go back the way you came," God said (v. 15). Elijah was to head north to Damascus and appoint three key men to places of leadership: Hazael (to be king of Aram or Syria, Israel's enemy), Jehu (to be king of Israel), and Elisha (to succeed Elijah as prophet).

These three men would change the course of Israel's future. Elijah did not live to see the major changes, but as he let the Lord lift him out of his depression, through him God set the wheels in motion to accomplish through Elisha what Elijah had not accomplished. As for Elijah's own future, boy, did he have one. He outlived King Ahab and was miraculously swept off to heaven in a chariot of fire (see 2 Kgs 2).

Rx for Depression

Has depression stopped you in your tracks? Consider the remedy given Elijah. Talk to God. Tell him where you are. Rest your body. Be open to receiving nourishment and sustenance from God's messengers; this might include friends who can share your load for a season, minister God's healing touch. Eat the food that will restore your physical strength. Get some more rest. Don't be afraid to go through the normal human process of grieving for your loss. As you do, listen for the gentle whisper of God. Allow that assuring, calm voice to restore your hope and your perspective. He can lead you to a new focus away from self and circumstances to a sovereign God and the meaningful future he's planned for you.

The Second Mile

1. Have you ever "crashed" after a mountaintop experience? Why does this happen?
2. Read 1 Kings 19. Have you had a similar experience of God's therapy (meeting physical, emotional, and spiritual needs) during a time of discouragement or depression? Explain.
3. Think of your current situation. Has "it's hopeless" slipped into your mind-set? If so, identify in one sentence exactly

what you feel is "hopeless." Is this perspective realistic, or have you lost some "perspective" along with your hope?

4. Elijah was convinced he was as good as dead. But that was not his only option. Try to identify two scenarios that might negate the "hopeless" scenario you identified in question 3. Now identify the first step you must take to move toward either of these two alternative options.

5. What are some of the key spiritual truths Elijah learned about God through his bout with depression?

6. How would you rate the apostle Paul's ability to resist depression in the midst of adverse circumstances? Read 2 Corinthians 4:8-9.

7. What seems to be Paul's secret in responding the way he did? Read 2 Corinthians 4:16-18.

8. Rephrase Paul's secret in your own words, making it "your own."

how can we feel close
when you're so near?

Samson: The Hunk Who Couldn't Find Intimacy

For the story of Samson, see Judges 13–16.

Those gray boxes with the blinking lights that sit on or by our desks are wonderful machines. We call them computers, and we use them to schedule appointments, balance our checkbooks, draw genealogical charts, map out trips, write letters, and even play games. In fact, the uses for this marvel of integrated circuitry and semiconductors are so broad not even industry pioneers Steve Wozniak, Steve Jobs, and Bill Gates together could have envisioned all the applications.

As creative minds develop phenomenally useful, labor-saving devices, however, we quickly learn to abuse them. Only three or four years after IBM introduced its first personal computer, someone found the new product could be used for "computer sex." At first it was bulletin-board explicit "conversations." Today, of course, we've progressed technologically. I understand you can find most anything in cyberspace, except the *real* thing.

Some people gravitate to virtual or keyboard relationships

simply because they are impersonal. You never touch a real person. In chat rooms, you can't be sure your correspondent isn't concealing his or her real sex, age, or personal interests.

So why are we talking about the sordid, explicit sexual conversations two total strangers can click out on their computer keyboards? It's because Samson, the Danite judge of Israel, would have fit right in with this cybersexual underbelly of computerized communication. Had Samson been our contemporary, I'm sure his modem would be smoking.

Perhaps you think I'm being unfair, so let me put it another way. Suppose we were on a committee to make a list of Old Testament men and women with outstanding spiritual qualities. We'd quickly nominate Abraham and Sarah, Isaac, Jacob, and Moses. We might add Joseph, Joshua, Gideon—and Samson? What if Samson's name came up? Would you vote for him? "No way!" comes a voice from the other end of the table. "He was a wise-cracking womanizer."

Actually, it's too late for a vote. The list has already been made, and in Hebrews 11 you can peruse the names. Verse 32 says, "And what more shall I say? I do not have time to tell about Gideon, Barak, Samson, Jephthah, David, Samuel and the prophets." There's that name, right along with David, Samuel, and the prophets! What's more, in the Book of Judges where we read about Samson, Gideon gets three chapters and most of the other ten judges don't get even one. Our questionable hero gets *four* (chapters 13–16).

So why is this man-on-the-edge (all his encounters with women are X-rated) given such prominence? Is there something God can teach us from the tragic story of this dysfunctional Hebrew Hercules?

Samson's Special Qualities

Samson's birth was surrounded by miracle and mystery. Like Isaac, Samuel (his contemporary), and John the Baptist, Samson's birth was associated with special circumstances. The angel of the Lord told a barren woman that she would bear a son. He was to be consecrated to God from birth and would attempt to deliver Israel from forty years of Philistine oppression. When Manoah, the woman's husband, heard the astonishing news, he realized that special blessing brings special responsibility. He prayed one of the most touching prayers of the Bible. "O Lord, I beg you, let the man of God you sent to us come again to teach us how to bring up the boy who is to be born" (Jgs 13:8).

The angel did appear again, generally repeating what he had previously said to the mother-to-be. The angel specified that the boy-child was to be a Nazirite. This special commitment to God involved avoiding four things: alcoholic beverages, unclean food, contact with dead bodies, and, yes, barber shops. The angel specifically told the mother-to-be herself to observe two of the prohibitions: Abstain from alcoholic beverages and don't eat food considered unclean. This is not bad advice for any pregnant woman, but here the prohibitions have special significance. (The wording hints that all four may have been applicable to her.) Apparently God was asking this woman temporarily to accept and model virtually the same Nazirite vows her son was to assume for life.

Judges 13:24-25 says that Samson "grew and the Lord blessed him, and the Spirit of the Lord began to stir him while he was in Mahaneh Dan." The account of Samson's life mentions the Spirit of God coming upon him. This was an unusual Old Testament occurrence, but it happened five times to Samson. First just a stirring at Mahaneh Dan. Later God's Spirit manifested himself through Samson's famous feats of superhuman physical power.

Samson also had a quick mind. The narrative repeatedly records his ability to adroitly adjust to new situations. Lacking a sword to defend himself, he picked up the jawbone of an ass and, as Israel's deliverer, killed one thousand Philistines. Even in the final tragic scene of his death, he was able to get the best of his captors in a seemingly impossible situation.

His wit is another evidence of his intelligence. It seems he was a master at riddles. What's he describing here? "Out of the eater, [came] something to eat; out of the strong, something sweet" (Jgs 14:14).

The thirty guests at his wedding feast would not have solved it, except that his bride betrayed him. Their answer sounds like the inspiration for TV's quiz show *Jeopardy:* "What is sweeter than honey? What is stronger than a lion?" Lest this seems nonsense to you, Samson had earlier killed a lion with his bare hands and later found the lion carcass filled with a swarm of bees and their honey.

Besides this riddle, a punny poem by Samson is also preserved for us in Judges 15:16. After putting down his battle-bloodied jawbone, he said:

With a donkey's jawbone I have made donkeys of them.
With a donkey's jawbone I have killed a thousand men.

A Loner Without Intimate Relationships

But there's a dark side to Samson's humor. It often seems to have been a thin veneer of civility hiding deep feelings of hostility. Samson liked to play with people, to hold them at arm's length. In fact, Samson was a hostile loner who was never able to establish lasting, intimate relationships.

That's still a problem many of us experience today, and it's especially endemic among single men and women I've known. A *McCall's* magazine survey some years ago asked twenty thousand women: "What is most important to you now?" Sixty-one percent answered, "A feeling of being close to someone." To the question "What is the ideal lover?" most men replied, "Someone I could be open and honest with."

There is a normal conscious or unconscious longing to experience the interlocking of personalities that we call intimacy. It's a psychological union, with a friend or mate, a shared identity that makes us together more than we could be if we each faced life alone.

Sometimes we're aware of the need, and we struggle toward this coveted closeness; at other times the barriers (we'll look at them later) are so great that our battle, like Samson's, is almost futile.

With Parents

I sense this lack of genuine intimacy in relationships, which was to blight Samson's whole career as Israel's leader, started at home in his relationship with his parents. One day Samson ventured into enemy territory, where he noticed an attractive Philistine woman. Back home he barked, "I've found the girl

I'll marry. Make the arrangements."

His parents protested weakly. They knew they were the ones who should make the arrangements, but they also knew they should also make the choice. "Get her for me!" Samson commanded. "She's the right one" (Jgs 14:3).

In Samson's defense we must note that the next verse indicates that this marriage was meant to provoke a fight with Israel's oppressors, the Philistines. Nevertheless, is this any way to treat your parents, affronting them with an order that made Samson the parent and them the children? Why didn't he confide in them and share his feelings? He could have said something like, "I know this is a little unusual, Mom, but it's OK. This is of the Lord. It's time to start my career as Israel's deliverer."

This wall of secrecy between Samson and his parents seems to be the principal characteristic of this unhappy parent-child relationship. When he accompanied his parents on their trip to arrange his marriage in Timnah, he killed a young lion with his bare hands. Did he share with them this remarkable demonstration of God's power in him? Scripture clearly says he didn't.

Later, when he found a honeycomb in the carcass of that lion, he gave some of the honey to his parents. Again we're expressly told that he didn't tell them where it came from. In this case his silence is a little more understandable. In touching the lion's carcass, he had broken one of his Nazirite vows. (Self-sufficient loners share their weaknesses and failures least of all.)

With Colleagues

Samson had similar difficulty in relating to his fellow countrymen. He fought his battles alone. Seeking revenge at one point, he managed to destroy Philistine fields of ripe grain, vineyards, and olive orchards. You would think he would have mustered an army to accomplish this formidable task. Instead he himself loosed 150 pairs of foxes into the Philistine fields. He tied their tails together, attached a flaming torch, and let them wreak a fiery devastation. In retribution the understandably unhappy farmers killed Samson's bride and her father. Then Samson single-handedly attacked and killed many of them, retreating to a rocky stronghold.

The Philistines reacted by marching north with an army to capture Samson. They were met by Jewish forces who, when they understood the situation, sent three thousand of their own men to capture Samson and hand him peacefully over to the Philistines. With friends like these, who needs enemies? Once again Samson failed to develop a relationship that would marshal his people into a cooperative effort to liberate Israel from their foreign oppressors.

The scene that follows in Judges 15 is almost comedic. Samson's countrymen approached the cave where he was hiding. "Hey, Samson. We know you're in there. Come on out. We need to talk."

Samson stood in the opening of the cave. "What do you want?"

"What do we want? Are you insane? Don't you know the Philistines are our rulers?"

"Not if I can help it. I just did to them what they did to me."

"Please come on out. We want to tie you up and hand you over to the enemy."

Here's a great chance for some fun, Samson thought.

"Promise you won't kill me before you hand me over?"

Is this for real? Israel's liberator was so "close" to his countrymen that he had to ask if they intended to kill him! Samson came out and meekly allowed himself to be bound by the men who should have been loyal to his leadership. Did they suspect anything? Didn't they yet know the cunning of this fellow they had in their hands? As they approached the Philistine camp, the Spirit of the Lord came upon Samson in power. He snapped the ropes. Here's where he picked up that jawbone and single-handedly slaughtered a thousand Philistine men.

With Women

This problem of intimacy with parents and peers is cause enough for worry about Samson, but there's more. His relationships with the three women in his life sharpen considerably the damning picture of his inability to experience intimacy. Take the young woman he demanded as his wife after he saw her in Timnah. She betrayed him in giving away the answer to his riddle, and for that he abandoned her even before their honeymoon. It seems she was just a dupe for Samson's forays against the Philistines.

When he decided it might be appropriate to consummate his marriage, he returned, only to find that her father had given her to Samson's best man. You know the rest of the story. He sent fox-tail torches to burn the fields. And then in revenge for that, the Philistines killed his wife and her father.

With this tragic beginning in Samson's relationship with women, things only got worse. He not only liked to use women; he liked to play with them. Going to Gaza, thirty-five miles into Philistine territory, he engaged a prostitute. Was he just trying to provoke another encounter with the enemy? (If so, it worked; keep reading.) Or was he, like many singles who have difficulty establishing lasting intimate relationships, tricked into accepting the pseudointimate?

News of Samson's whereabouts traveled fast. The townspeople schemed to ambush him at dawn. Finally they'd grab their man. Unfortunately this is the kind of situation Samson thoroughly enjoyed. He liked to walk as close as he could to the edge of danger. What better way to show how cleverly he could make an impossible escape?

In the middle of the night, he left the woman and left his mark: He tore loose the city gates and carried them to the top of a nearby hill. If he couldn't do real damage, he would at least prove his superiority and cunning as Israel's leader.

Then there was the fabled Delilah. She may have been Samson's true love, but he could not escape the pattern he had established for his life. Nothing drew them together in the intimacy that is supposed to characterize the relationship of a loving man and woman. A substantial Philistine bribe prepared her to betray him from the very outset. As for Samson, even though he said he loved her, he used her. He lied to her. He played with her—hardly secure foundations for a growing, intimate relationship leading to marriage.

Three times Delilah asked Samson for the secret of his phenomenal physical strength. He easily could have explained it was God working in and through him. Instead, he offered imaginative, untrue explanations, quite aware that the enemy was waiting to render him powerless and kill him. "Tie me up with seven thongs, and I'll lose my strength." They tried it. It didn't work. "Tie me with new ropes." It didn't work. Three times he escaped. Then, tragically, he stepped a little too far over the line that separates excitement from security. "Cut my hair and ..." That night, sleeping with his head in the lap of the woman he said he loved, Samson got his first haircut.

Telling Delilah about his Nazirite vow never to cut his hair was perhaps Samson's only real attempt at intimacy. But his attempt at drawing close to her was done so poorly that it ultimately cost him his life. He failed because he put his closeness with a person ahead of his closeness to God. It backfired. It backfires every time you or I try it too. It always will.

A Humiliated Hero

As for Samson, the Philistines "seized him, gouged out his eyes and took him down to Gaza," where they bound him in bronze shackles and "set him to grinding in the prison" (Jgs 16:21).

In time Samson was dragged out as entertainment for a great celebration of thanksgiving to the Philistine god Dagon. After all, the Philistines had captured Samson, their great enemy.

In the midst of that mocking crowd, the blinded, humiliated hero prayed the only prayer we hear from his lips. "O Sovereign Lord, remember me. O God, please strengthen me just once more, and let me with one blow get revenge on the Philistines for my two eyes" (v. 28). Again with brute force, he pushed down the two load-bearing pillars of that great building. The temple of Dagon collapsed on Samson and the dignitaries inside. What's more, there were three thousand spectators on the roof. In this single, vengeful act, he killed more of the enemy than he had during his whole lifetime. And in a final stroke of irony, his body was buried between Zorah and Eshtaol; that's where the Spirit of God had first come upon him.

A tragedy? Yes, a tragic death and a tragic life too. For twenty years Samson was God's appointed leader, charged with freeing Israel from the oppressive rule of Philistia. As the angel prophesying his birth said, "He will *begin* the deliverance of Israel from the hands of the Philistines" (Jgs 13:5, emphasis mine). Samson was the last of the twelve heroes we call judges, and his unfinished conquest of the fierce Philistine oppressors was left for Saul, Israel's first king. Saul succeeded in providing some protection for his people, but it was King David who finally brought the troublesome coastal nation to its knees some eighty years later.

It's interesting that God knew Samson's limitations even before he was born. He would *begin* the liberation of Israel from Philistia. God chose him anyway. God used him, flawed as he was, to the fullest extent of his abilities. Isn't that encouraging?

Removing Barriers, Building Bridges

Yet I grieve for Samson as I grieve for singles today who somehow fail to see how they might be putting up barriers to the close relationships God wants us to have with himself, with family, friends, and even possibly a mate.

Here's a concise list of some of the barriers to intimacy identified by a group of single friends. They also skillfully listed actions that can be taken to move closer to God, to people, and to the full potential God has for us in serving him—what we called bridges to intimacy.

Barriers	Bridges
Lack of communication	Learn to share feelings
Rejection, fear of looking stupid	Dare to take risks
The Lone Ranger mentality	Accept a dependent role
Unrealistic expectations	Lower expectations
Disloyalty	Support others
Selfishness	Maintain a spirit of giving
Taking others for granted	Invest in maintaining a relationship
Lack of forgiveness	Forgive
Intolerance	Accept others as they are
Inflexibility	Be willing to change

Let's briefly look at the first two of these barriers, as they're closely related. What the singles in our discussion group meant by *communication* was, more precisely, self-disclosure. Do we let people into our lives? Sometimes our barriers are high. Sometimes we only indirectly give information about who we are. For example, if I tell you I like maple bars, you will learn a little about me. But if I tell you a bakery in my hometown used to unlock the front door at 6 A.M. just to sell me a hot maple bar before I started my paper route, I've indirectly told you how very important those bars were to me.

Charles M. Sell, in his most helpful booklet called *Intimacy: The Wonder of Drawing Close*, defines self-disclosure as "sharing your intimate feelings, inner thoughts, and desires." We rightfully shouldn't go around indiscriminately sharing our inner lives with everyone. There are appropriate and inappropriate levels. With new acquaintances we first relate facts, then interpretations of facts. More intimate conversation reveals feelings and emotions. But some of us never get to sharing feelings and emotions. This is especially true of men.

Note this comment by David Smith, author of *The Friendless American Male:*

> Even when men are frequently together their social interaction begins and remains at a superficial level. Just how long can conversations about politics and sports be nourishing to the human spirit? The same male employees can have lunch together for years and years and still limit their conversation to sports, politics, and dirty jokes and comments about the sexual attractiveness of selected female workers in their office or plant. They do not know how to fellowship.

Yes, some men simply "don't know how" to talk about feelings. And, particularly for singles, such conversation can be misinterpreted. Getting beyond the superficial might be received as an indication of interest in romance. Perhaps romance will be the result, as friendship buds and blossoms, but certainly friendship comes first. Carefully chosen words, topics, and, above all, body language will help you clearly convey the I-just-want-to-be-friends message.

But let's admit that some of us share very little of ourselves with anyone because of the second barrier to intimacy: fear of rejection. We are afraid of being "discovered," as Charles Sell puts it. He suggests several reasons for this fear, including the following.

"Shame" and "unworthiness." We're convinced that there's something wrong with who we are. Shame is usually seen as being different from guilt (for specific actions). Shame makes us think that there is something broken in us that can't be fixed. We're nobody. Worthless. And afraid to let anybody find out about it.

The image factor. We simply want to be perceived as being "together," "perfect," as if we were always on a first date. Again it can be reduced to: *If they find out who I really am, will they reject me?* True intimacy becomes impossible until this deceptive posture is dropped and our faults are acknowledged.

How do we walk toward intimacy? My singles' group identified the "bridge" as being willing to take risks in our relationships. "Do I dare?" we ask ourselves. Perhaps a better question would be, "Dare I *not*?"

"There can be no intimacy without risk," Charles Sell reminds us. "Unless I reveal myself to others, they are not accepting me as I am: they are accepting an illusion of me."

Here are three suggestions that can help you move toward intimacy in a relationship without opening yourself to the trauma of huge embarrassment, should your friendship not be accepted. Again, I've summarized these from Charles Sell:

1. Take "just one step" beyond what feels utterly safe and comfortable. Easy does it. Don't go deep, or stay there a long time, until the relationship begins to mature. On the other hand, if you feel no discomfort, you're probably still at a very superficial level of self-revelation. Telling someone who you are *is* scary.

2. Cultivate a sense of timing. If you share too much too soon, or under inappropriate circumstances, your friend or potential love may be pushed away, rather than drawn closer.

3. Be sure to accept the other person's thoughts and emotions. This acceptance and support is a powerful incentive to continue the relationship and move to still greater intimacy. Are you *listening* to and for the other person's thoughts, feelings, and desires? Or are you just projecting your own agenda for this relationship?

As you peruse the list of barriers given earlier, try to discover the one that constitutes the highest, thickest wall between you and the warmth of the intimate relationship you long to enjoy. Look at the corresponding bridge that could carry you over this wall. Do the needed changes seem easy, difficult, impossible?

Don't despair. Building intimacy is a skill to be cultivated, to be learned. I've known some singles who rationalized like this: "The pain of staying the way I am is less than the pain that would be brought by the changes I need to make." So they stayed the way they were. Lonely, unfulfilled, unable to realize the wonderful potential God had for them.

Others, on the other hand, looked at themselves and agreed with Howard J. Clinebell Jr., in *Intimate Marriage*, when he observed, "It takes a major investment of energy to maintain the distance and keep the barriers intact...." Wouldn't we rather use that energy to tear down the barriers and put in some bridges?

Life and Death in the Dark

Samson died in the dark, a blind man. But even before the Philistines had gouged out his eyes, hadn't he lived in darkness—blind to the weakness he never seemed to recognize or try to overcome? How much more he could have accomplished had he learned to trust and work with others!

How about you? You were designed for intimacy with God and with the people around you. The need is great and so is the temptation to settle for pseudointimacy that never satisfies and can lead to disastrous, long-term consequences.

The road to intimacy starts with your relationship with God, whom Scripture calls "a jealous God" (Ex 34:14), who does not want to be second to your relationship with any person or thing. The God who empowered Samson for those incredible exploits of physical endurance and power is the same God who can strengthen you by his indwelling Spirit. With this spiritual power you can break away every barrier that hinders you from experiencing the intimate relationship he wants you to have with himself and others. It's not the easy way, but it's the way of joy. It's the way that God can prepare you to be used to your fullest potential.

The Second Mile

1. If God uses involvement with himself and others to help us grow, what would be the result of experiencing only shallow or perfunctory relationships? Why?

2. While recognizing Samson's weaknesses, it's important to realize that it was God who chose him for an important ministry. In Judges 13 what evidence do you find of this divine appointment?

3. Based on reading Judges 13, what kind of a career would you have predicted for Samson?

4. What evidence do you find in Judges 14 that Samson's motivations for marriage are something less than "true love"?

5. Have you ever "used" people to further your own agenda or even God's work? How do you feel about this?

6. Do you ever use humor, as Samson did, to keep people from getting too close? How can laughter be used to draw people closer?

7. In the final chapter of Samson's life, a haircut symbolizes his broken commitment as God's servant. Can you think of a symbolic act that could have similar significance for a Christian today?

8. How do you think a more intimate relationship with God and others might change your life? Read 1 John 1:5-2:6 and see what this intensified intimacy might cost you.

9. We know God chose Samson. Is it possible that God also chooses you and me, with all our imperfections, to use us for his glory? As you answer, consider the prayer in Ephesians 1:3-10. Personalize Paul's prayer for the Ephesians by changing the pronoun *us* to *me* and *we* to *I*.

the way to a man's heart is not through his left ventricle

Ruth: The Widow Who Found the Recipe for Remarriage

For the story of Ruth, see the Book of Ruth.

Trim, prim widow, twentyish, seeks new friendships since relocating from the southeast. I'm loving, determined, industrious, and loyal. If you're into computers or sailing, that's OK, but if it's backpacking, don't ask. I'm seeking the comfort and joyful companionship of a godly, older, Jewish gentleman who is financially secure, kind, intuitive, romantic, decisive, and willing to father the special children I'm longing to have. If this sounds good for starters, let's meet for a picnic in the country. We may be able to glean some ideas that will uncover a great and exciting future for us both. P.O. Box 77, Bethlehem, Judea.

The biblical Ruth would never have written an ad like this, of course, but every week thousands of men and women do. Marriage and remarriage: It's the single itch that won't go away. And it's spawned a thriving industry. Affection Connection classifieds, cruises, books, and other commercial enterprises compete with one another to help Cute Christian or

Hunk-Lover to hook up with Fun Cowboy. One national video dating program even promises to make singles' bars obsolete and save you valuable time in getting into a loving relationship. "You will never have to date 'nice,' but 'not-your-type' people again!" the brochure says.

As with any hankering, there are levels of intensity. In chapter one I mentioned Myrna's ultimatum: "If I don't have a husband in thirty days, it's good-bye church, good-bye God." Less than a month later she brought in a quiet young man and introduced him as her new husband. Looking rather bemused, he greeted our group, and we haven't seen either of them since.

On the other end of the scale are the singles who think it's great to be free and have no intention of getting married or remarried. Some will change their minds as some inner pain, often of divorce, heals. Most singles, however, fall somewhere between these two extremes.

Worst Things About Being Single

I once asked a group of divorced men and women what was the worst thing about being single. Their responses were illuminating.

Men:

The collie I come home to can't talk to me.
My lousy peanut butter sandwiches.
Not seeing my children as much as I would like.
Having to do my own laundry.

No one to share life's responsibilities with.

Having to pick out someone to date.

Women:

The cruel discrimination of the government, married couples, and the church.

Having to use an electric blanket to get warm in bed.

No one to share a beautiful thought with.

No one to fix the roof.

No one to unstick a zipper.

No man to be around my boys.

The burden of having to make decisions alone.

Ruth's Sorrow, Ruth's Choice

Will marriage fix all these things? It's possible, but perhaps this isn't the question we should be asking just yet. Let's jump back in time about three thousand years to a young widow named Ruth. She didn't have to worry about electric blankets or stuck zippers, but she was finding life difficult in ways and at a level of intensity few of us have experienced. A triple tragedy had rocked the life of this Moabite woman and the lives of two people close to her. First her father-in-law had died, leaving Widow Naomi. Then Ruth's husband had died, as did his brother, leaving Ruth and her sister-in-law Orpah as widows.

Widowhood, never an easy load to carry, was nearly the end of the road for any woman in Ruth's day. Because a woman depended on her husband for financial security, his departure put his widow in an extremely vulnerable position. This passage and many like it deal with the problem head on: "Do not take advantage of a widow or an orphan. If you do and they cry out to me, I will certainly hear their cry" (Ex 22:22-23). Other Old Testament passages promise God's care and protection for foreigners, orphans, and widows (Ps 68:5; 146:9; Is 55:4-5, for example).

The solution for Ruth and Orpah, according to their mother-in-law, Naomi, was remarriage. And the custom was for a widow to marry her deceased husband's brother. But Naomi had no other sons; not even a husband ... and at her age.... Pessimist that she was, she viewed Ruth's remarriage as being a remote, even impossible, scenario. "Am I going to have any more sons, who could become your husbands?" she asked (Ru 1:11).

When faced with unbearable, unsolvable circumstances, we lie awake at night going over our options. That's what Ruth must have done at this juncture. Naomi, an Israelite, announced she was going back to her home country, to Bethlehem. Ruth could stay in her native Moab, where she grew up, where her husband was buried. There was no other man on the horizon, but at least she would be in the familiar culture with her own family of birth.

On the other hand, she could go to Bethlehem with Naomi. The famine that had driven Naomi and her husband to Moab seemed to be about over. Young Ruth could help Naomi survive as a widow. Would there be a husband for her in Judea? This uncertainty didn't seem to be Ruth's concern.

She may have had second thoughts about living with Naomi, who seems to have become a bitter, pessimistic old woman. She went around saying things like, "My troubles are worse than yours." "God is against me." Her bitterness had taken its toll. Ruth 1:20 says she even changed her name from Naomi (pleasant, agreeable, delightful) to Mara (bitter).

There must have been at least one other consideration as Ruth struggled to make this important decision to stay or to go. She was a Gentile. What sort of a reception could she expect in Jewish Bethlehem? Would she be doubly vulnerable as a widow and a foreigner? And what about this God of Naomi's? Would the Almighty make their lives "very bitter" in Bethlehem too?

Ruth weighed the pros and cons and made what seems to be a completely selfless choice. She and Orpah set out for Bethlehem with old Naomi. During the early part of their eighty-mile trek, Ruth's decision to stay with her mother-in-law was tested three times. "Go back to your mother's home," Naomi urged. "Go back to Moab." In a very emotional scene, the three grieving widows hugged and kissed one another, pledging their loyalty. Again Naomi painted a hopeless picture of their future without husbands and urged them to go back home. Orpah gave in and returned home. "Go back with her," Naomi urged Ruth a third time.

Ruth looked at her sister-in-law and hesitated, sorting through her options once again. *That's right*, Naomi thought, *choose her, not me. Choose your people, not mine. Choose your god, not my Jehovah.*

Ruth's reply to her mother-in-law is such a classic, all-embracing pledge of loyalty that it's become a standard part of many wedding ceremonies. "Don't urge me to leave you or to turn back from you. Where you go I will go, and where you stay I will stay. Your people will be my people and your God my God. Where you die I will die, and there I will be buried. May the Lord deal with me, be it ever so severely, if anything but death separates you and me" (Ru 1:16-17).

I don't know about you, but I'm with Orpah. *Naomi offered a graceful way out of a thankless, seemingly stupid choice, and I'm taking it. Life with bitter old Naomi is going to be one huge ordeal.* That's the only apparent certainty in Ruth's uncertain future, so how do you explain her decision?

Selfless, unconditional love is the only motivation I can come up with to explain Ruth's astonishing choice. There were none of the usual provisos such as, "I'll stick with you as long as …" or, "I won't ever go back to Moab if you promise to …" Ruth's loyalty is pretty hard to understand when we look around us and see a culture today that seems totally pre-occupied with promoting the what's-in-it-for-me? syndrome. Perhaps the key to Ruth's heroic decision was her Jewish husband. He wasn't around very long, but he may have reflected God's love in his relationship with Ruth and his mother. Selfless love can be catching.

At any rate, Ruth and Naomi said their tearful good-byes to Orpah. She turned and headed east toward Moab; Ruth and Naomi resumed their journey westward toward Bethlehem, Naomi's hometown. A crotchety old woman and a vigorous and loving young woman—about to begin a new life together.

Considering Marriage?

I want to interrupt Ruth and Naomi's story to introduce a framework of sterling qualities I see emerging in Ruth. These are issues I see as important for any woman desiring marriage or remarriage, as is the case with Ruth. As we walk through Ruth's story, let's identify some principles for decision making in regard to marriage. They are really written from the petticoat side of the junction, but male readers too may glean some helpful ideas about approaching remarriage.

Her Preoccupation

Ruth was no Myrna. Remember Myrna in our Sunday school class, verbally shaking her fist in God's face and demanding a man? Ruth's pledge to stand by Naomi until "death separates you and me" indicates that Ruth's focus was on selfless service, not on romance. And as we shall see, she was serious in her commitment.

Her Plan

Settling into her new life in Bethlehem, Ruth seemed unaware that a man in her life might solve a lot of her problems. She was just thinking survival—putting the next meal on the table and coping with a depressed old woman who, at least for the moment, had given up on life and on God. In the biblical narrative, one little detail reminds us that she had no plan for building and baiting a man trap. When she went out to glean enough barley for their next meal, she just *happened* to end up in the field belonging to Boaz, a close relative of her mother-in-law (see Ru 2:3). And surprise! We've already met Boaz's mother and father in another chapter: Rahab from Jericho and her Israelite husband Salmon.

Ruth's gross lack of strategy stands out in sharp contrast to the contemporary scene. I think of the book *The Rules*, Ellen

Fein and Sherrie Schneider's best-selling paperback that promises to provide readers with "Time-Tested Secrets for Capturing Mr. Right." Their strategy is based on carefully calculated manipulation and misrepresentation. According to the authors, the man of your dreams will not notice he's being tricked if you follow their thirty-five guaranteed rules of behavior and misbehavior. So "as long as you don't outright lie, you needn't be honest to a fault, either." Jim Shea, reviewer for the *Idaho Statesman* (February 14, 1997), feels the "underlying philosophy is based on the premise that ... a woman can trick a man into chasing her—until she catches him."

Did Ruth manipulate this older, well-to-do Jewish farmer into marriage? I don't see it that way. Here's what I see as Ruth's principle in this regard: She had no time or inclination to build a devious matrimonial trap.

Her Person and Reputation

Character played the dominant role in Ruth's remarriage. Her biblical story begins with a strong demonstration of her selfless loyalty. As the narrative continues, we see little glimpses of a very winsome personality. Was she pretty? We don't know, but there was something about her that caused Boaz to notice her among the workers in his field. "Whose young woman is that?" he asked his foreman (Ru 2:5).

I notice, too, Ruth's manner with Naomi and with Boaz's foreman. It's characterized by kindness and warm, unaffected courtesy. We've already seen her deferential treatment toward Naomi on their trip to Bethlehem. Once they were established in Bethlehem, before Ruth left the house to glean with other impoverished Bethlehemites, she asked her mother-in-law's permission. Permission granted, she found a field being harvested. "Please let me glean and gather among the sheaves behind the harvesters" (Ru 2:7a). The foreman told Boaz of this well-mannered woman, and Boaz responded in kind.

Ruth was courteous, and she was also a hard worker. The foreman continued his report to Boaz: "She went into the field and has worked steadily from morning till now, except for a short rest in the shelter" (v. 7b). And Boaz gave her specific permission to glean in his fields and to drink from his water jars.

Have you ever known a person in great need? You try to help, but that person won't let you? The problem is stubborn independence, pride. Ruth wasn't like that. She humbly accepted help when it was offered. Acutely conscious of her foreign birth and all its ramifications, Ruth realized she had no claim to the special treatment Boaz offered. But she accepted it graciously. "Why have I found such favor in your eyes that you notice me—a foreigner?" (v. 10). Boaz's kindness mystified her, but she graciously accepted it all.

If she wondered at Boaz's special attention to her, Ruth didn't have to wonder long. As far as he was concerned, her outstanding trait was her reputation (vv. 11-12). For good or bad, our reputations often arrive before we do; with one like Ruth's, there was no need to worry. Boaz saw her as a caring single woman who had made considerable sacrifice to come to the aid of her widowed mother-in-law.

We've seen that Ruth was a woman who remembered to say please. She didn't forget to express her appreciation either. "May I continue to find favor in your eyes, my lord. You have

given me comfort and have spoken kindly to your servant"
(v. 13).

Boaz invited her to eat lunch with his workers. And then we
see a glimpse of *his* goodness. He told his harvesters to leave
behind a little extra for Ruth and, whatever you do, "don't
embarrass her" (v. 15). Ruth's sterling qualities were beginning to make a powerful impression on the man who would
soon be popping the question.

So let me summarize the "stuff" that made Ruth the person
she was. Both appearance and character played a part. That
included good manners, a humble spirit, a good reputation,
and sincere expressions of gratitude.

Her Patience

This is one of the qualities I admire most about Ruth, probably because I've watched so many singles ignore calendars and
even clocks in their romances. The ink is hardly dry on the
divorce papers before they are compulsively signing a new
marriage license.

There's not a hint of any impetuous action on Ruth's part.
The narrative tells us that she and Naomi got back to
Bethlehem early in May at the start of the barley harvest. Ruth
continued her work in the fields until the wheat harvest ended
in June. Two months seems like a long time to wait to make
your move, especially when a highly eligible male is paying you
special attention. Dating hadn't been invented yet, so Ruth
and Boaz were getting acquainted with each other as they
worked together.

Not a bad idea. Dating has its place, but there's a certain
artificiality in the typical evening out where everyone is look-

ing good and on his or her best behavior. Try tackling a sweaty work project with your friend, together with other singles. How does this man behave around other women in an informal setting? How does he relate to men? How does he deal with the irritations, the unexpected, or challenging problems?

Ruth's secret here was taking the time to get acquainted with the new man in her life in a setting that would reveal a great deal about him.

Her Awareness of Her Vulnerability

I see Ruth as vulnerable on three counts: She was still grieving as a new widow; she was a woman in a man's world; and she was a stranger in a new culture. Here are three caution lights that ought to warn anyone. Be aware of these and any other points of vulnerability that could inhibit wise decisions in developing new relationships.

Grieving people are not noted for making rational decisions. It's a wonderful time for unscrupulous people to move in and get what they want. My friend Marty learned this the hard way. It's almost beyond belief, but an attractive woman proposed to him at his wife's funeral. Soon afterward they married, quickly found they had made a terrible mistake, and divorced. The experience was educational, to say the least, but the emotional scars may never go away. If you've faced a major loss, don't jump quickly and impulsively to sell the house or move to get away from it all or find a new mate. Give yourself time. Give God time to heal your wounds.

Sadly, just being a woman makes one vulnerable. Interestingly, Boaz and Naomi seemed quite aware of this problem for young Ruth. Even on the property of a close relative, Ruth seemed to have been in potential danger. "Don't go away from here," Boaz cautioned her. "Stay here with my servant girls…. I've told the men not to touch you" (vv. 8-9). Then back home again with her bulging barley bag, Ruth told Naomi she'd been working in a field belonging to Boaz. Naomi approved. "In someone else's field you might be harmed" (v. 22). The tragedy in the singles' scene is that vulnerability is sometimes accompanied by naiveté. The combination can be lethal.

As for Ruth's vulnerability as a foreigner, I can certainly identify with that problem after twenty-five years as an alien in Brazil. Inevitably you sometimes get taken advantage of or misunderstood just because you don't really understand what's going on.

During our first year in the country I was struggling to learn Portuguese. Carmozina, our pastor's wife, graciously consented to correct my teaching notes. In my cultural ignorance, I almost destroyed her reputation and mine. I wrote on note-sized paper so it would fit in my Bible. A neighbor child usually took the pages down the street to Carmozina's house. She would make the necessary corrections and send the papers back with one of her boys. Village tongues began to wag. Weren't we exchanging *billets-doux*? (This was the accepted courtship device before dating became acceptable.) And didn't we sometimes spend a lot of time together in intense conversation?

Even Carmozina was caught off guard. One afternoon I arrived at her house to find our principal detractor awaiting my arrival. I handed her the "love letter" Carmozina and I were about to review. She studied it carefully, handed it back, and finally left without a word. Only then was the problem resolved. I still remember the disappointed I-could-have-sworn-something-was-going-on-here look on her face.

Are you, in fact, in a vulnerable situation? It's unlikely that your circumstances will be identical to Ruth's. The point is to look for things that could cause vulnerability and result in choices that drag you down the road to tragedy. Are you on the rebound? Have you just moved, changed jobs, or been seriously ill? These are just a few yellow caution lights to look ahead for.

It's difficult to know what the time span is in the little Book of Ruth. She was in Bethlehem at least long enough to establish a good reputation among the villagers.

But we can be sure that she took all the time necessary to become well acquainted with her new environment and the man who made her think about marriage.

Her Preparedness

Ruth was prepared to do her part to reel in a catch when the proper time came. Her Jewish mother-in-law helped her act at the proper time. The harvest was finally over and threshing had begun. Naomi was so low-key in her approach, it makes me smile. "Should I not try to find a home for you where you will be well provided for?" (Ru 3:1). I can almost imagine Ruth looking at the aging woman hobbling toward her, smiling back, and saying, "Interesting you should mention it, Mother. I was just thinking the same thing about you!"

Completely out of character, of course. Ruth would never have said that. Instead, she heard Naomi's plan. *The waiting game is over. It's time for lights, camera, action!* Not exactly.

Although there's not even a tiny hint of impropriety, this was to be an after-dark, undercover operation. No more sweaty, harvest work clothes either. It's good-bye grubbies and hello perfume and a pretty dress. If Boaz had liked Ruth before, he was about to wake up and discover he had not been dreaming.

The ancient Jewish marriage customs that follow are strange to us, and we can hardly expect to understand them fully. In fact, by the time the Book of Ruth was written they had become obsolete in Jewish culture. It's sufficient for us to notice that flawless timing and absolute secrecy were essential to the success of Naomi's plan to bring Ruth and Boaz together. Nowadays secrecy doesn't seem such an essential, but timing continues to be a fierce feminine tool.

It was the end of the workday. Boaz had rested, had a good meal, had a little to drink, and he was happy. It would seem that Boaz was the vulnerable one at this point, as Ruth crept around the pile of grain to where he was sleeping, gently pulled the cover up off his feet, and lay down to wait. Apparently she was saying, *I'm available for marriage if by any chance you're interested.* Something startled him and he woke up. He was flattered that she had not "run after" younger men. There was a whispered agreement. Ruth lay down at his feet again, and he shared a corner of his blanket.

To maintain the secrecy that's so essential to completing this kinsman-redeemer marriage arrangement, Ruth and Boaz were up before dawn. He put six measures of barley in her shawl, and they went their separate ways back to Bethlehem.

A closer relative, who had right of first refusal for a family plot of land, wasn't interested in the land when he realized that Ruth was included in the deal. Just what Boaz had hoped!

The land—and Ruth—could rightfully belong to Boaz. The complicated deal was witnessed, and Ruth became the wife of Boaz.

You too may be thinking how wonderful it would be if a Prince or Princess Charming appeared on the scene. Are you ready if one does? Are there loose ends to tie up before you slip on the ring? Are there debts, other sorts of unfulfilled obligations, schooling, or professional or personal growth that need to be taken care of? When God's candidate for marriage appeared, Ruth was ready.

Her Promise

The last quality I notice about Ruth is her continuing faithfulness. The pledge she made to Naomi on the road to Bethlehem did not end when Ruth married. In fact, it was intensified. "Where you stay, I will stay" became "Where I live, you will live."

I can hear the two women talking as they make preparations for the wedding. "Naomi, I talked with Boaz last night," Ruth says. "He has this big house on the other side of town, you know. We're getting a nice room ready for you."

"Your people will be my people" was to be a reality in the most intimate sense possible. Ruth married into her Jewish mother-in-law's family in Bethlehem.

Many details of Ruth's story show that she meant "Naomi, your God will be my God" with all her heart. But both women died without ever understanding the unique, far-reaching meaning of those words. Ruth was King David's grandmother, and, if you follow the Davidic lineage on through the New Testament (see Mt 1), you see that Ruth was an ancestor of Jesus, the Messiah.

It was true for Ruth, and I hope it's true for you: Promises made to those you love do not end with marriage.

Recipe for Remarriage?

"OK," you say, "that was God's way for Ruth, but it all happened a long time ago. I'm not so sure it would work today."

It will work. Follow Ruth's model of selfless loyalty, patience, and hard work, and you'll become the person God wants you to be. That's the priority for all of us.

Will this recipe always put all the ingredients together to produce a wedding cake? Of course not. We men are so stupid. We look for all the wrong things in a woman. Beautiful legs; a swelling bosom; gorgeous, kissable lips. The deep spiritual qualities that make you a godly, blessed woman may be quite invisible to all but a few very special men. As unconvincing as it may sound in hours of intense loneliness, being unmarried may be far better than finding a partner who does not value you for what you are in your deepest, most precious dimension, the spiritual.

Sharon was one of those rare catches. She was intelligent, she was fun, and her deepest desire was to please Jesus Christ in everything she did. She was already a spiritually mature woman before her marriage collapsed. God used that hard experience to bring even greater spiritual depth in her life.

At our weekly singles' meetings, Sharon was always there to do what no one else thought to do. She greeted newcomers, served refreshments, and freely gave of her time and wisdom for our steering committee. My wife and I kept wondering why some of the men in our group didn't wake up. Yes, she was a little overweight and had three kids. Yes, she plucked her eyebrows so she could paint them back on, but what a jewel!

Finally there was a flicker of romantic interest from one of the men in our group. Sharon and Dick became steadies. Some thought they were made for each other; others thought he wasn't good enough for her. They were close to being engaged when the welfare of her children proved to be more important than remarriage. Sharon's teenagers had serious difficulties accepting Dick and were drifting into behavior patterns Sharon couldn't control. She decided to move to a small rural community up north where she hoped teen temptations would not be so readily available.

Some of us thought Sharon was making a big mistake to leave her home, her church, and a community where she had a job and was well established. She believed she knew what God wanted her to do, so she didn't pay any attention to us. She packed up and left.

Our singles' group was never quite the same after we said good-bye to Sharon, but she saved her kids. After they left home and were well established, she went off to Bible school, graduated, and went to Europe as a missionary. After a few years of service, she injured her leg, had surgery, and died from unexpected complications.

I'm glad Sharon didn't pin her future on the appearance of the Mr. Wonderful who would treasure her spiritual maturity. She used everything God gave her to give back to him. I'll see her in glory someday, and I know what I'm going to say:

"Sharon, I was wrong. You did the right thing in saying good-bye to all of us—and to the romance you were so ready for."

The Second Mile

1. The story of Ruth is set during the chaotic period of "the judges." It is a warm ray of sunshine that burst out from behind a dark historical cloud cover. What does this suggest to you about the way God works?

2. Ruth's decision to go to Bethlehem with her mother-in-law was a selfless choice in the extreme. Have you ever chosen the best for someone else when it could well have been the worst for you? How did it work out?

3. Most divorced or widowed singles I know want to remarry. I suspect Ruth did too, but her selfless service as she waited for Mr. Right seems quite atypical. Do you think this is so? Why?

4. "Rules girls" are encouraged to conceal facts about themselves that might nip a blossoming romance in the bud. Although Ruth had a few negative qualities (foreigner, widow, poor), news about her seems to have spread quickly throughout her village. Do you have information you want to hold back when you enter a new environment? Why?

5. If you were to write some "God rules" for dating based on the Book of Ruth, what would they be? Write three for men and three for women.

6. How does Ruth happen to go to Boaz's field? Is it because she is a man-hungry, scheming widow? Discuss your reac-

tion to the following quote from *Quest for Love* by Elisabeth Elliot: "If we imagine that happiness is to be found by furious pursuit, we will end up in a rage at the unsatisfying results. If, on the other hand, we set ourselves to pursue the wide and loving and holy will of our Heavenly Father, we will find that happiness comes—quietly, in unexpected ways...."

7. Which of Ruth's true-hearted qualities do you have?

8. Write an Affection Connection ad that stresses your spiritual qualities.

9. Don't miss the blessing of rereading Ruth's ancient romance. While you're at it, see if you can find the *eight* benedictions in the book. (A benediction is a blessing one person gives another.) Could you write blessings for three people you care about? Slip them into envelopes and get them into the mail today.

caring enough to care

Jonah: The Single Who Couldn't Feel Compassion

For the story of Jonah, see the Book of Jonah.

My wife, Julie, has a favorite childhood story she likes to recall when someone with the best intentions (usually me) manages to bungle a seemingly elementary assignment. Epaminondas, the little boy she read about in third grade, was like that. His mother would give him simple, clearly defined instructions, and he always had a terrible time carrying them out. As she remembers it, one of his misadventures went something like this:

Epaminondas' mother told him to hurry over to his grandmother's and bring home some butter. It was a very hot day, so his mother gave him a piece of string and said, "Tie this string around the butter, and tow it along in the stream on your way home so it won't melt."

Unfortunately for Epaminondas, the butter wasn't ready when he got to his grandmother's. "I haven't had time to churn," his grandmother said. "I'll get you a cookie, and you wait while I churn the butter."

"I can't stay," Epaminondas remembered. "Mother said to get right back home."

"Well, all right," his grandmother said. "But so you won't go home empty handed, let me give you that little puppy I promised."

Epaminondas picked the prettiest little puppy from his grandmother's newly weaned litter. He tied the string his mother had given him around the pup's neck and started back home. When the path crossed the stream, he remembered he hadn't fully carried out his mother's instructions. He tossed the dog into the water and towed the poor little animal down the stream until he got home.

Looking out the kitchen window, Epaminondas' mother saw the little boy pulling the half-drowned pup out of the creek. She sensed immediately what had happened. "Epaminondas!" she exclaimed (as she always did), "You haven't got the sense you were born with!"

My wife doesn't remember how this children's book (probably no longer politically correct) ended, but we can hope Epaminondas finally did learn to use "the sense he was born with."

Of course not all of us do. Our parents pound on us while other teachers try to get our unwilling minds to focus and apply. Once out of school we have an employer to help us try to get things straight. For the more recalcitrant, sometimes there's an officer in blue or a black-robed judge to exert additional pressure in our educational process. God, it seems, has a way of bringing just the right circumstances into our lives to help us learn the particular truths he sees as essential to our lives and ministry.

At least that was the way he worked with a prophet named Jonah. I'm not sure Jonah ever got to prophets' school; if he did, he struggled through several basic courses. You would have seen them listed in the fall catalog as Obedience 101, Prayer 101, and Compassion 101.

Obedience 101

Let's review how Jonah actually flunked Obedience 101. God told his servant to go to Nineveh and preach: You're so wicked … prepare to die. God knew the people there would be responsive, that his missionary to the capital of the Assyrian empire would be instrumental in one of the greatest revivals the world has ever seen. But instead of heading northeast, eight hundred miles around the fertile crescent to Nineveh, Jonah decided to go almost to the western edge of the known world. He boarded a ship sailing for Tarshish, a city in Spain, three thousand miles in the opposite direction.

We always go to extremes, don't we, when we try to run away from the Lord? What do we have to do to get out of the sight of an omnipresent God? Pull down the blinds? Turn out the lights? Move to another city? Change jobs?

Perhaps Jonah, standing there on the dock at Joppa, was like some singles I've known. They like to brag a little bit about their mobility. "Don't have a dog. No wife, no kids. I can just pick up and *go.*" No doubt this freedom is a great advantage, but it can be abused. With time, money, and freedom of choice, Jonah headed for Tarshish, the place of escapism, self-determination, and possibly self-indulgence.

Nineveh, the destination he dreaded, was the place of usefulness and the astonishing out-working of God's sovereign plan. Have you checked your compass lately? Make sure yours and God's are both pointing the same direction.

Jonah, like many of us who consciously decide to disobey God, rebelled because he didn't see what God saw. Jonah saw great danger in the east, and he was afraid. Don't forget, the powerful Assyrian empire was Israel's archenemy. The biblical prophet Nahum, who later prophesied the city's destruction, characterized Nineveh as a "city of blood, full of lies, full of plunder, never without victims!" (Na 3:1). So we rationalize: "What's better, Lord, a dead obedient prophet or a live disobedient one?" We forget that obedience rarely brings martyrdom to anything but our own selfishness.

Jonah 4:2 indicates that Jonah also had a problem with pride. After all, a man of God has his reputation to maintain. Suppose he were to go and preach divine judgment to the Ninevites. Suppose they were to repent. Suppose God in his mercy spared them. *How am I going to look,* Jonah must have reasoned, *when my prophecy doesn't come true? With us prophets, you know it's one strike and you're out.* Is this the way you handle God's message? Does your reputation sometimes get in the way when it's time to speak the truth in love? Are you a people pleaser or a God pleaser?

Prayer 101

Another required course in the school of prophets was Prayer 101. Fortunately for him, Obedience 101 was offered again the second semester—this time along with a course in prayer.

That second round of classes started out with a storm so violent the classroom was about to break up. Jonah was on the ship to Tarshish. Jonah's classmates, an ungodly bunch, were all so scared that they started to pray. Not Jonah. He was in the back row, his head down on his desk, sound asleep.

I've thought a great deal about Jonah's emotional state in the first chapter of this highly condensed narrative. (The entire Book of Jonah is only about two pages long.) I think he was exhausted and deeply depressed. His self-esteem was off the scale, and he just might have been suicidal. He'd sobbed until he couldn't sob anymore. He knew he was going the wrong direction, but his ship was committed to its course, and there didn't seem to be anything he could do about it. Well, there was something God could do about it. And he did.

My son-in-law has a couple of high-spirited, blue-ribbon pudelpointers. They don't look like much, because every day is a bad hair day for them, but because they cost a lot and are exceptional hunting dogs, David doesn't want to lose them. Unfortunately the feeling is not mutual. When he lets them out for a run, the most insignificant distraction will start them putting distance between themselves and home. You can yell their names with "come!" as long as you want, but they will be gone, perhaps not to reappear until the next day.

The solution for this problem is called a shock collar. The collars pick up a radio signal from a transmitter in the owner's hand, and the dog receives a quick electrical shock. David hates to push one of those buttons, because he knows it hurts his dogs. He also knows a mild shock will stop their flight and bring them home—usually. There are actually four levels of intensity. If they don't respond to the mildest, the voltage can be stepped up a notch. When the dogs do not respond and are out of sight, David pushes the red button. The dogs receive a continuous shock until he sees them racing toward home.

What do you think? Does God sometimes deal with us the way David deals with his disobedient dogs? We don't respond to his voice, so he alters the comfort level of our circumstances. If that doesn't get our attention, he makes additional changes until we feel them and head for home.

Here's Jonah, the second time around in a class on obedience and also enrolled in a course on prayer. He's awake now. Everyone's been praying but the prophet. Would he fail the course? All good teachers know their main job is to motivate their students to learn. I can just imagine the Master Teacher's thoughts as he planned some special motivational techniques for his most stubborn student. *Let's see ... solitary confinement in a hot, dark, smelly little room for as long as it takes.*

You've probably got all the usual excuses for not praying as you know you should. Too busy. Not enough faith. Doesn't make any difference. What would it take to get you started? Would you dare to begin by praying what Jesus' disciples prayed—"Lord, teach us to pray" (Lk 11:1)—and then not complain if instead of a pattern to follow, he brought circumstances so difficult that you couldn't *stop* talking to him?

That's what God lovingly did for Jonah. The sailors knew they would all die unless the storm abated. Who was responsible for the storm? The roll of the dice indicated it was the disobedient, prayerless prophet. The waves grew higher, and in desperation and profound guilt, the sailors accepted Jonah's offer to let them toss him overboard.

A big fish just *happened* to come alongside the foundering ship at the exact moment Jonah sank into the raging sea. Gulp! What a place to have a prayer meeting! God found a surprising way to get Jonah through Prayer 101. His technique worked so well that he gave his vertically challenged student an A+.

In Jonah's prayer from the belly of a great fish, he acknowledged that he was near death. He knew he was helpless to do anything about it. He realized his need for God and abandoned his independence.

And then, not surprisingly, his values and priorities changed. Serious prayer has a way of doing that. "I said, 'I have been banished from your sight; yet I will look again toward your holy temple'" (Jon 2:4). In other words: "I ran from you and here I am, about as far away as any man can get. I don't like it. I'm ready to obey and look east now, just as you told me."

A little later Jonah added, "Those who cling to worthless idols forfeit the grace that could be theirs" (v. 8). Apparently he'd learned in a practical way what he may have known only theoretically in chapter 1, where he introduced himself to the sailors: "I am a Hebrew and I worship the Lord, the God of heaven, who made the sea and the land" (v. 9). Jonah could use a little of that dry land right now, and God in his grace was about to give it to him.

Jonah's long weekend seminar on prayer was over. The giant fish found the prophet to be quite indigestible. God gave a command only fish could understand, and Jonah was deposited rather messily on the shore.

As we've seen, Jonah passed the course on prayer. He was also about to ace his final in Obedience 101. Did he learn to obey because God made his task easier? Or because the rewards were greater? Or because he knew everything would turn out all right in the end? No, everything was just the same—except for the heart of God's servant.

Jonah changed because he learned a few other things besides how to pray and how to obey. He found one really can't hide from God, and if one could, one wouldn't like it. (That's what I like about education: We discover the things we don't like to do as well as the things we enjoy.) Jonah also discovered that God's plan for our lives cannot be frustrated. Further, he learned in a very practical way that (surprise!) disobedience brings discipline.

Compassion 101

So far, Jonah's grade-point average looked very good, but he still had one final class: Compassion 101. Jonah's classroom moved east to Nineveh. He was now on the street, preaching, and his message was simple: "Forty more days and Nineveh will be overturned" (Jon 3:4). If that's all there was to it, he could have said that short phrase in Assyrian with hardly an accent.

But if the message was simple, the results were spectacular. The whole city believed God's message. Every level of society fasted and put on coarse, baglike garments. It was a symbolic announcement of the people's grief over sin and their repentance. Even the king took off his royal robes, put on sackcloth, and sat in the dust. "Let everyone call urgently on God," he said in a proclamation. "Let them give up their evil ways and their violence. Who knows? God may yet relent and with compassion turn from his fierce anger so that we will not perish" (vv. 8-9).

Right here I'm most disappointed that Jonah's story is so briefly told. How do you explain such revolutionary results from such a simple, brief pronouncement?

We probably don't have the whole text of Jonah's sermon. But if the people really believed what the prophet said, the issue was one of life or death. Why on earth should the Ninevites have given credence to this disturbing message from an unknown foreigner?

I think they would have believed for several reasons. First, let me explain a little about their god. Asshur was the supreme god in the Assyrian pantheon. He was their Mars, the god of war. The Assyrian king was his high priest and representative. Over time, Asshur had taken on the characteristics of other gods. In the Assyrian myth of creation, he even assumed Marduk's identity in his momentous battle for supremacy against the fierce sea monster Tiamat. Asshur won his battle against Tiamat. When she opened her mouth to swallow him, he had the power to force hurricane winds down her throat; incapacitated, she died from a fatal Asshur-shot arrow.

Stay with me; that sea-monster story may prove significant.

Now, let me give you an idea of what Jonah might have looked like, having spent seventy-two hours sloshing around in the gastric juices of an aquatic monster. Fortunately, numerous accounts of "sea monster eats man; man survives" have been recorded in modern times. In one striking, authenticated account reported by Gleason Archer in *A Survey of Old Testament Introduction*, one James Bartley disappeared when his whaling boat was overturned by the lash of a sperm whale's tail. But the whale was caught, and two days after killing the whale, having removed the blubber, fishermen removed and opened the whale's stomach. Inside they found a "doubled up and unconscious" Bartley. He was revived with a "bath of sea water." After three weeks he was back at work, fully recovered, except that "his face, neck and hands were bleached to a deadly whiteness and took on the appearance of parchment."

Now we're getting the picture! Here is a Jewish street preacher on his three-day preaching tour down the streets of Nineveh. People hear his message and laugh. But when they ask him about his strange appearance, the laughing stops. Here is a man who, unlike their supreme being, Asshur, actually was swallowed by their sea monster Tiamat. Although helpless and unarmed, he subdued her and was freed from his visceral prison.

"You don't believe me?" Jonah must have said as he looked around at the incredulous stares of the people on the street.

"Are you saying you are more powerful than our lord Asshur?"

"No way," Jonah would have answered. "My God is powerful to destroy; he's also powerful to save. He delivered me from the sea monster. You want proof? Look at my face, my neck, my hands."

The result? By the time Jonah finished his three-day crusade, tens of thousands of Ninevites were on their knees begging Jonah's God for mercy. And Jonah, the undisputed Billy Graham of Assyria, wasn't he thrilled with the phenomenal response to his altar calls? *Au contraire, Pierre.* Jonah was about to start another class, this time in compassion.

He had passed the remedial stuff. This course was more

difficult, and it was going to be a struggle. A lab course, conducted right in the field. Jonah couldn't believe it when God said he wasn't going to destroy Nineveh. "When God saw what the [Ninevites] did and how they turned from their evil ways, he had compassion and did not bring upon them the destruction he had threatened" (v. 10).

At this Jonah was outraged, grossly offended. But he was ready to apply what he had learned in Prayer 101. Do you mind if I put my own words in his mouth?

"Now you've gone and done it, Lord! Yes, I ran away. You know why? I was afraid of this. I knew you really wanted to save these horrible people, not exterminate them. What kind of a God are you, anyway, to do this to me?"

He crouched down in the little brush arbor he'd made to the east of the city where, just to be sure, he'd camped out to see what God might do. *I'll give the Lord a second chance to do what I think he ought to do.* Jonah was a basket case—extremely depressed and suicidal. There's no time to waste, Lord. Let's get this class started!

As recorded in this little book filled with miracles, God planted a seed and a vine shot up and covered Jonah's crude arbor. Our compassionate God provided a little extra comfort from the blistering desert sun for his distressed servant. Jonah appreciated the extra shade (though he may have thought he'd mistakenly enrolled in some kind of an agricultural course).

The next morning, when the bell rang and class started, a big fat worm slithered into the classroom. The worm hadn't had breakfast, so he chewed down the succulent vine Jonah had been so grateful for the day before. The vine withered and died, and Jonah felt the heat of the midday sun, exacerbated by a searing Santa Ana wind. Jonah grew faint, on the verge of a heat stroke. The dialogue that follows, Jonah talking with the Teacher, is choice. Jonah spoke first. Was he about to fail the course?

"It would be better for me to die than to live."

But God said to Jonah, "Do you have a right to be angry about the vine?"

"I do," he said. "I am angry enough to die."

But the Lord said, "You have been concerned about this vine, though you did not tend it or make it grow. It sprang up overnight and died overnight. But Nineveh has more than a hundred and twenty thousand people who cannot tell their right hand from their left, and many cattle as well. Should I not be concerned about that great city?"

JONAH 4:9-11

In the Book of Jonah, God has the last word. That's the end of the story. There's no verse 12. God's last word to Jonah is, *Get beyond your own pity party and understand the depths of my compassion. You yourself have been the recipient of my great mercy. You headed in a disastrously wrong direction. I spared your life. I taught you to pray. I spared your ministry. I spared you from the blistering heat. I took away the vine only to get your attention. Now, are you ready to live in and live out my compassion?*

If we assume that Jonah himself wrote the book that bears his name, he did ultimately show a commendable grasp of theology. He recognized God's grace, compassion, patience, and mercy. But as he demonstrated earlier, it's not enough to have a truth in your head. It has to be in your heart for it to work in everyday life.

When you understand compassion only in your head, for instance, it's fine when God deals with *you* lovingly. (It's fine when he sends a shading vine on a hot day.) The problem comes when he chooses to deal in mercy with someone you deem to be unworthy of his care. Think in terms of the parable of the Prodigal Son. You become like the disapproving older brother standing off to one side as the loving father welcomed home his wayward son. Or, if you prefer, you become like a Pharisee criticizing Jesus for the kind of people he associated with.

On the other hand, if you have a heart-understanding of God's compassion, you allow him to extend it to anyone he chooses. You may even allow him to use you to be the messenger.

Years ago, when our singles' group was new and small (we hardly knew what a singles' ministry was supposed to be), there was a special quality evident in our share-and-prayer times. One Tuesday evening a dozen of us were comfortably seated around our host's living room. A young woman we'll call Jean was across from me on the couch, giving us a litany of her terrible week. Her ex-husband was intensifying an already unbelievable campaign to make her life as miserable as possible. A problematic, developing romance was adding its measure of stress. We'd heard it all before, and, frankly, some of Jean's problems were of her own making. Some of us were wondering if she really deserved our sympathy and help.

Jean began to weep. She struggled to talk through her sobs, then finally just totally gave in to the emotion. Sounding more spiritual than I felt, I said, "Let's pray right now." As we bowed our heads, I saw Betty dash across the room and sit on the floor close to Jean. She took Jean's hands in hers and prayed as if Jean's problems were her very own.

I don't think there was a dry eye in the room that evening as Betty invested a little of her life in the life of her sister. I don't think she realized it, but she also gave me a much-needed lesson in compassion.

In his book *The Ragamuffin Gospel,* Brennan Manning says, "Compassion for others is not a simple virtue because it avoids snap judgments—right or wrong, good or bad, hero or villain: it seeks truth in all its complexity. Genuine compassion means that in empathizing with the failed plans and uncertain loves of the other person, we send out the vibration, 'Yes, ragamuffin, I understand. I've been there too.'"

I've obviously never forgotten Betty's gesture of compassion toward Jean. I fear this incident that happened more than twenty-five years ago is so memorable because it's all too rare. Is our track record to those outside the church any better than with our brothers and sisters in the faith? Theologian Francis Schaeffer looked at the church from the perspective of the tumultuous sixties, but there is still truth in his insight, that the church has a way of alienating particular groups of people, not deliberately but through "an enormous lack—of compassion."

We are driving the young away from us in school, in our churches, and very often even in our families. If they are different from us in the smallest detail, even the most unimportant and unessential detail, we shut them out. We have no love, no compassion for them unless their life styles match ours.

In his article "Christian Compassion: Have We Lost Our Touch?" (*Eternity*, December 1970), Schaeffer went on to illustrate what he meant by compassion, using the ministry at his Alpine retreat center, L'Abri, as an example. In the first three years after he and his wife opened their doors, his needy guests "wiped out" all their wedding presents. Bedding was torn, holes burnt in rugs, and drugs were brought into their home. People vomited in their rooms. Allowing things like this to happen so people could be reached with the gospel was the true meaning of compassion, Schaeffer said.

Suggestions for Class Projects

Listen to God's direction in your own circumstances. I don't know his particular plan for you. But here are a few suggestions for projects in your own class of Compassion 101. As you listen, pray, and obey, consider this insight offered by Steve Sjogren in his book *Conspiracy of Kindness:* "Our job is to be seed flingers, not seed protectors watching over God's business as though he had a limited supply" of seed, of love, of compassion.

The easiest place to start a "compasssion" project is within your singles' group. We once had a large bulletin board and posted the kind of headings you might find in the classified section of a newspaper: Card of Thanks, For Sale, Wanted to Buy, Help Wanted, and so on. Singles filled out three-by-five cards and pinned them under the appropriate headings. Help Wanted was by far the most popular with the ladies. Tasks such as a garden to spade, a faucet to fix, or a fence to mend were offered in exchange for a pie or a home-cooked meal. I don't guarantee it for you, but for us some of these cards brought people together permanently.

Other kinds of projects can reach beyond the group. They can include evangelism, social outreach, and world missions, as Jimmy Long suggests in *Small Group Leaders Handbook*. "Evangelism could mean encouraging friendship evangelism in [or outside] the group, having an evangelistic Bible study or book table, or doing contact evangelism. Social outreach could include visiting a nursing home, painting a house, participating in hunger relief projects, or sponsoring blood drives."

Does a visit with a person who is old and alone seem formidable? (Someday it might be you; many single people are terrified of growing old alone.) Ask this older person for insight on how to have a good life. What does she most value having done? What does he most regret? Get them talking. Leave them with a smile and a prayer for God's compassion and mercy to be shown to them.

World missions could include sponsoring a short-term trip, praying for missions, or making yourself available to provide for the special needs of a missionary family.

The Second Mile

1. Did Jesus accept this strange little story of a stubborn prophet and a big fish as historical fact? (Read Matthew 12:40.)

2. Is there any sense in which you can run away from God? Explain.

3. What technique has God found most effective in your life for getting you to do what he wants? Give an example.

4. Do difficult times drive you to pray more? Why?

5. Jonah is a book filled with miracles. How many can you find?

6. What circumstances has God used in your life to teach you that:

   a. you really can't hide from him?

   b. disobedience brings discipline?

   c. his plan for our lives cannot be frustrated?

   d. God is compassionate and merciful to you?

   e. God wants you to show compassion to others?

7. Name one way you plan to show compassion to someone in the next twenty-four hours. In addition, be on the lookout for an unexpected opportunity to show God's love.

hanging super tough when the going gets rough

Daniel: The Single Who Had the Courage of His Convictions

For the story of Daniel, see Daniel 1–6.

Sociologists seem to like to categorize and label us according to generational characteristics. The forty-three million or so folks born between 1927 and 1945 are called the Builders. They're a pretty traditional bunch when it comes to values. They've got money (although few went to college), and they tend toward an America-right-or-wrong perspective.

Then we have the Baby Boomers, that phenomenal spike on the population graph that told us World War II was over and our men were home from Europe and the Pacific. This much maligned and misunderstood group has a reputation for greed and self-centeredness. They see their careers as the central focus of their lives, and leisure time is used mostly for self-improvement.

Generation X, sometimes called Baby Busters, are the Jasons, the Tiffanys, and the Todds born between 1965 and 1978. Forty percent of them are children of divorce.

I suppose sociologists were well-meaning in their efforts to give us all names. Marketing specialists have certainly benefited. They've gone into a feeding frenzy trying to tailor their products and services to the characteristics of a given generation. As for the rest of us, we now have precise names for the group we most fervently dislike.

Take the Builders and the Boomers, for instance. Builders have a strong work ethic and they live in their own homes. They may have attended a church of the same denomination all their lives. It is hard for them to understand the Boomers who are restless, moving all the time, looking for something more suitable. Why do they keep avoiding long-term commitments?

The biblical Daniel would not have understood the Boomers. Daniel was a Builder. His values were traditional, and he would have scratched his head in disbelief at the seeker mentality of the Boomers. "Why waste time looking when I've already found it?" Daniel would have asked. He worked hard, sought to excel, and was one of the few of his generation who made it to college. And incongruous as it may seem, this leader from the Jewish elite living in exile in Babylonia seemed to believe it was "Babylon right or wrong."

Not that life was easy for Mr. Commitment. It seemed that powerful forces in the godless Babylonia would test him almost until the day he died.

A Young Man With a Future

This brilliant, handsome teenager named Daniel landed in Babylon against his will. Babylonian forces from the northeast, led by King Nebuchadnezzar, put Jerusalem under siege. Judah's King Jehoiakim soon caved in and enemy troops swarmed into the city. Daniel, with a small group of Jewish elite, was probably taken to Babylon in the first of Nebuchadnezzar's four conquests of Jerusalem.

Daniel 1:3-5 indicates that Nebuchadnezzar ordered Ashpenaz, his chief of staff, to select a number of bright young men from the Judean nobility; they were to be sent back to Babylon to receive three years of special training, to enter the king's select service. Among that select group were Daniel and his friends, Shadrach, Meshach, and Abednego.

Once in Babylon, Ashpenaz may have said: "No time for homesickness or crybabies. You've got a new language to master, and you won't believe the reading list you're going to get. After all, this is the renowned Babylonia U."

Now here's the opportunity so many teens dream of. Get a job, get an apartment, get away to school. Anything to get out of Mom and Dad's sight! This doesn't seem to be the case for Daniel and his friends. They accepted and believed the values their parents had passed on to them. There was nothing they wanted to get away from. In fact, it was these values from home that were going to keep them on their feet when many others would have stumbled.

That was the first test of Daniel's commitment: *What are you going to do when Mom and Dad aren't breathing down your neck?* And the next? *What are you going to do in a godless, secular university?* Well, it wasn't exactly godless. I suspect this three-year crash course in language and "literature" involved a lot of pantheistic mythology. Today it would be something like a creationist taking a university course in physical anthropology under a confirmed Darwinian evolutionist. As a Christian you wouldn't be able to accept what you were being taught, but you would have to master the material and answer test questions as if they were gospel truth.

Daniel and his three friends apparently managed this problem with great skill. In fact, they graduated summa cum laude. It doesn't always happen that way. A pastor once lamented to a friend of mine that the "atheistic, secular humanism" lurking in today's university classrooms had destroyed the faith of one of his young people. My friend responded, "I guess he didn't have very much faith to be destroyed." Faith. That was the secret of these four Hebrew boys at Babylonia U. They had too much faith to be destroyed by an educational system I dare say was more of a threat than the secular institutions we sometimes fear today.

A superficial commitment to God and his ways was not Daniel's problem. His problem, early on, was that the food served in the student dining room didn't come from a kosher kitchen. "What did you expect?" asked Ashpenaz. "Mama's home cooking?"

For Daniel and his classmates, it was something far more than just preferring "Mama's cooking." Daniel and his loyal friends resolved not to "defile" themselves by eating the food set before them. Jewish law laid out many requirements that separated the ceremonially clean from the unclean. So if Daniel ate the king's food, he would in effect be repudiating his commitment to obey God and his laws.

This is a very delicate situation, and Daniel handled it with the maturity and skill of a much older person. Here's his predicament: He was, in a sense, a royal guest. A full scholarship, including full room and board with the very best cuisine—and he had to go and complain about the food!

Daniel proposed that he and his friends be served veggies. This left the field wide open, because Mosaic law did not designate any vegetable as clean or unclean. So you needn't feel too sorry for the boys from Jerusalem. They had an extensive menu to choose from. How about starting with a melon appetizer, followed by lentil soup? The main course: stuffed cucumbers garnished with onions and with just a touch of garlic. Then a bean dish with olives on the side, parched corn, barley bread with honey, and several kinds of nuts to munch on. For dessert, a choice of dates, raisins, fig cakes, pomegranates, or other fruits in season.

It helped that Daniel's supervisor liked him, but the proposal was not well received. This man was afraid the vegetarian diet would harm the boys' physical health and stamina. If this were so, what would the king do? The man might lose his job if not his head. Nevertheless, he conceded. At the end of the ten-day trial proposed by Daniel, he and his friends looked "healthier and better nourished than any of the young men who ate the royal food" (Dn 1:15).

Perhaps you, like me, are thinking that you might not have the courage to propose such an experiment. You want to please God, but let's not carry things too far! Remember, Daniel was a Builder—strongly traditional but willing and able to make a way and "make do." *If our food is bad, we can do something about it.*

The course at BU ended. Daniel and his friends not only survived, but they excelled. They mastered a new language, a new culture, all the course work the academics threw at them.

They were ready for their oral defense before the king. By the king's standards of comparison (his magicians and astrologers), it was no contest. The practitioners of monotheism rated ten to one over the priests of polytheism.

There are at least three things we can learn from young Daniel's story so far.

First, how can we combat the urge to violate our faith when we're far from home and no one is looking? Jerry Jenkins wrote some helpful advice about this in his book *As You Leave Home:*

> Too many people exercise their new freedom by relaxing their spiritual disciplines, dropping out of church for months, and becoming lax in their Bible reading. You will want to explore, to try new things, to expose yourself to a variety of worship styles. But do yourself a favor and make a pact, not with me or with God, but with yourself. Decide in advance that no matter how much church shopping you do, or what different things you try in the exercise of your faith, you will not put that spiritual life on hold even for a season.

Daniel didn't and we don't have to either.

Second, besides this pact with yourself, you might also try making a different kind of contract with trusted friends you see regularly. In *The Trauma of Transparency,* J. Grant Howard offers this practical counsel: "A friend told me he was struggling with the temptation to read pornographic literature. He said, 'When you meet me during the week, ask me how things are going, and we will both know that you have reference to this area of temptation. Just knowing that you are going to ask about it will stimulate me to resist the temptation.'"

Second, how can we resist the pervasive forces that seek to bend our minds? A godless world is seeking to educate us—formally and informally—to press our minds into its man-centered molds. We become so intrigued by its siren call that we, like the ancient Greek mariners, risk shipwreck, hardly realizing that we're being seduced.

The lure to draw us into the rocks will always be with us. Our defense must be consciously to develop a Christian worldview. How do we do this? The answer is complex, but in *The Making of a Christian Mind* author Arthur Holmes suggests that one of the fundamentals is solid theological concepts. "We need a biblical understanding of God as Creator and Lord of all, and of our place as persons bearing God's image, in creation, sin and redemption. These will undergird, indeed they give rise to, a Christian view of art or science, work or play, or anything."

Finally, how can we withstand cultural pressures that try to push God out of our lives? Culture must never be our arbiter of what is right or wrong. It can only tell us "what's hot and what's not." And its choices usually have no regard for ethics or morality. We who take Daniel's stance against what is accepted as culturally correct will usually be swimming upstream. We need to remember that everybody is *not* doing it, and even if everybody were, that would not make it right or wrong.

Daniel's Gift, Support, and Prayer

We're getting ahead of the story. Let's backtrack, as does the biblical narrative. When Daniel was still an undergraduate at

BU, new circumstances arose that would determine once again what he was and what he wasn't. In fact, success would mean life; failure would bring death.

King Nebuchadnezzer had a troublesome dream. He was so disturbed he couldn't sleep. He called all his spiritual advisers—magicians, enchanters, sorcerers, astrologers. He insisted that they not only interpret his dream, but also—and first—tell him what he dreamed. The king was adamant about this strange request. His advisers (whom he accused of stalling for time, and they were) finally gave him their bottom line: "You're asking the impossible. Only a god could reveal the content of your dream." Outraged, the king ordered the execution of every wise man in the city. This included the wise-men-in-training, Daniel and his three friends.

What did Daniel say when they came to get him? "Please, I'm too young to die! I haven't even finished college yet"? No. Daniel's negotiating skills again came into play. He seemed fearless as he focused his considerable tact and wisdom on the executioner. "The king's decree seems a little harsh," Daniel suggested. "Do you suppose I could talk with him?"

Somehow Daniel persuaded the king that he had the ability to interpret the dream, but that he'd need a little time. Apparently the king had cooled off a little by now, and he granted a stay of execution.

When you have the skill and IQ of a Daniel, you're not apt to ask for help, but that was exactly what he did. When he got back to the dorm, he called his three roommates together for a prayer meeting. They'd received mercy from the king. Now they needed mercy from their God, for what the wise men had said was at least partly true: Only "the gods" could reveal the content of the king's dream. The only trouble was, the gods were remote and unapproachable.

Clearly, the true God was going to have to intervene in this crisis if there was to be a happy ending. Fortunately for Daniel, his God was accessible. After the prayer meeting the boys went to bed wondering, I'm sure, what God was going to do. How long would they have to wait before he answered their pleas? Would the king's patience hold out? Would they live through the next day?

Sometime during that night, God gave Daniel a vision that revealed the mystery of the king's dream. Daniel couldn't wait. He had an impromptu praise service. We aren't told that his friends joined in, but I hardly think it could have been otherwise. Who could have stayed asleep in that dorm room?

As far as we know, this was Daniel's first foray into dream interpretation. He eventually was gifted with interpretations and visions themselves, but first times are special. (See the second half of the Book of Daniel. We won't cover his visions in this brief study.) When experiencing these special, intimate encounters with God, I think sometimes it's a little hard to keep one's balance. After all, God could have chosen any one of the four Hebrews. I imagine Daniel thinking: *He chose me!*

I like Daniel's perspective. He knew he had a very unusual gift, and he knew exactly where it came from. The wisdom, this great intellect that was to make him useful all his long life, came from God.

I like to listen to people talk to God. When they're really praying and not just mouthing pious platitudes to try to impress those around them, you can learn so much about people. Daniel's prayer impresses me in several ways. There was balance, perspective, and a whole lot of wonderful, mature theology. If he had previously learned these facts about God, he certainly was grasping them also in his heart. Read his prayer, found in Daniel 2:20-23.

Prayer	*Theology*
Praise be to the name of God for ever	*God is eternal.*
and ever; wisdom and power are his.	*God is wise and powerful.*
He changes times and seasons;	*God is sovereign.*
he sets up kings and deposes them.	*God is all powerful.*
He gives wisdom to the wise and	*God is generous.*
understanding to the discerning.	*God is wise.*
He reveals deep and hidden things;	*God knows everything,*
he knows what lies in darkness,	*especially what is hidden to mankind.*
and light dwells with him....	*God is light.*
You have made known to me what	*God hears and answers prayer.*
we asked for.	

Come morning, Daniel was granted an audience with the king. Perhaps it's easy to have the proper perspective in the privacy of your own room. Let's see if Daniel can keep his humility and balance in the presence of one of the most powerful men of his world.

"No wise man, enchanter, magician or diviner can explain to the king the mystery he has asked about," Daniel began (v. 27).

"Yes, Belteshazzar (Daniel's Babylonian name), I think we've already established that. I'm going to kill the lot of them. Go on."

"But there is a God in heaven who reveals mysteries. *He* has shown King Nebuchadnezzar what will happen in days to come" (v. 28, emphasis mine).

Actually, I think Daniel's claim to a personal connection with the supernatural was not a surprise to the king. All his wise men were presumed to do things that were beyond human powers. One of their most common functions was to secure secret knowledge, especially information about the future. What must have been a shocker to the king was that Daniel was identifying his God, the Jewish God, as his source of information. Why would Jehovah show special favor to the man who was about to destroy Jerusalem, the Holy City, and Solomon's magnificent temple?

Whatever God's reason, Daniel recounted the king's dream: an awesome image of a man made of gold, silver, bronze, and iron. The dream was of great interest to Nebuchadnezzar because it depicted kingdoms. As head of the world's superpower, that's all he thought about. As Daniel explained it, each metal depicted the rise and fall of an empire. The gold head was Nebuchadnezzar himself. Each kingdom would in turn be smashed by a "rock cut out of a mountain, but not by human hands." Finally, "the God of heaven" would establish his own kingdom over which he would rule forever (vv. 44-45).

Nebuchadnezzar's response to Daniel's ability to recite and interpret his dream must have stunned the young student. The king recognized Daniel as a kind of demigod. The king bowed before him and ordered that incense and an offering be brought to him. He also gave him many additional gifts and an upper-level government job.

It's hard to imagine Daniel standing still for all this. He

knew who he was: God's servant first, not the king's. Any special ability he had came from the true God and not from some magical expertise that linked him to the false gods of Babylonia.

Somehow Daniel stood firm. He even remembered his roommates who knelt with him in prayer to plead for God's mercy. At Daniel's request, the king made them provincial administrators.

Daniel must have also tactfully said something that convinced the king he could not accept his worship. The king backed off and came close to making a confession of faith: "Surely your God is the God of gods and the Lord of kings and a revealer of mysteries" (v. 47). This is quite a statement from a king known for his inscriptions of hymns and prayers to the gods of the Babylonian pantheon. Further developments show, however, that whatever conviction he felt about the true God was only temporary.

Before we go on, let's take five and try to make sense of all this. Daniel has great courage, negotiating skill, and an unusually mature dependence on God. We can explain some of this simply by remembering that Daniel was an extraordinary young man. The rest, I think, has to do with Shadrach, Meshach, and Abednego, his three dorm mates at Babylonia U. This was his support group; these were his accountability partners. They talked things out; they prayed and praised the Lord together. These four young men were soon to go their separate ways, but at this crucial time their association was essential for survival.

Are you going it alone on one of life's bumpy roads, about out of gas, and wondering how you'll reach your destination? You need to be part of a small group where people you love and trust can pray for you, give strength and stability. If your church doesn't have an opening in such a group, start your own. I started mine by extending just a casual invitation. My single friend Norm and I have been studying and praying together for about a year now. It worked for Daniel. It works for us.

Respectful Employee

When next we are allowed to look in on Daniel, he's an alumnus of BU. He's in his thirties or forties, a trusted, well-established governmental leader in Nebuchadnezzar's palace. The king's final military campaign against Daniel's hometown, Jerusalem, is long since complete. A major deportation has brought thousands of Jews to Babylon. They are well established in their new world as exiles.

In Daniel 4 we see Daniel looking up from his papyri-cluttered desk, because the king has had another bad dream. Daniel tells us about it by letting us look at an edict written by Nebuchadnezzar himself; as we read it, we see he's still talking a good talk. "How great are [God's] signs, how mighty his wonders! His kingdom is an eternal kingdom; his dominion endures from generation to generation" (v. 3).

It's logical that he should talk like this, because he's recalling the miraculous deliverance of Shadrach, Meshach, and Abednego from the fiery furnace. After their deliverance the king had professed a similar allegiance to Daniel's God. "Praise be to the God of Shadrach, Meshach and Abednego.... They trusted in him and defied the king's command and were willing to give up their lives rather than serve or worship any god except their own God" (v. 28).

In his enthusiasm he followed through with an edict: Anyone who said anything against the Jewish God would be chopped to pieces and his house leveled.

Still, when a crisis befell Nebuchadnezzar, he followed old habit patterns. Instead of calling Daniel, who supervised the astrologers and magicians, he called his discredited spiritual advisers. It's a dangerous thing to see the truth, acknowledge it, and then turn your back on it, as Nebuchadnezzar was about to discover.

When Nebuchadnezzar asked for an interpretation of his nightmare, the "wise men" didn't have a clue. He had dreamt of an enormous, beautiful tree that was then felled and stripped of its branches. There was something about a stump. Something about seven.... Finally he turned to Daniel, who understood the dream's symbolism but was afraid to reveal God's interpretation. Only after Nebuchadnezzar encouraged him to speak up did Daniel interpret the dream: Nebachudnezzar was the great tree. He would fall and be stripped of his glory, but the stump (what remained of him) would be preserved and after "seven times" he would return to power. More specifically, the king would go insane and live like an animal in the field before regaining his sense and his kingdom.

The tragedy was that even after repeated nudgings, Nebuchadnezzar's recognition of the true God had not gone beyond lip service. Daniel told him, "Your kingdom will be restored to you when you acknowledge that Heaven rules" (v. 26).

Daniel ended his interpretation with hope and respect: "Therefore, O king, be pleased to accept my advice: Renounce your sins by doing what is right, and your wickedness by being kind to the oppressed. It may be that then your prosperity will continue" (v. 27). Possibly Daniel was thinking of his own exiled people as he boldly confronted the king with his accusations of injustice.

As it turned out, Nebuchadnezzar had a year to heed the wisdom of Daniel, now his chief administrator. Then one day he strolled on the palace roof and boasted of his power and glory and majesty. "Is not this the great Babylon I have built ...?" (v. 30). Zap! The people drove their suddenly crazed king out of the palace and into the fields, where he lived like an animal, until his sanity was restored after seven "periods." Utterly humbled, he then praised God, acknowledging him as eternal, sovereign, and omnipotent. Remember Daniel's midnight prayer of thanksgiving? These were the same characteristics of God that Daniel himself had acknowledged. Perhaps ultimately Nebuchadnezzar learned about God through Daniel's words and exemplary life.

The Writing's on the Wall

Let's look at another episode in Daniel's life, recorded in Daniel 5. God did restore Nebuchadnezzar to his throne for a time, but eventually his son Belshazzar became king. Daniel, the faithful civil servant, was now in his seventies. Belshazzar had been on the throne for fourteen years. He wanted to throw one of the most memorable parties of all time. He invited a thousand of the country's rich and famous to the palace banquet hall. Let the party begin. Belshazzar had one of those brilliant ideas half-soused people sometimes come up with. "This calls for a special toast. For our ladies—bring in the golden goblets Daddy looted from the Jerusalem temple. I want them to drink too!"

As they continued in their unrestrained indulgence, they toasted their gods of gold, silver, bronze, wood, and stone. Suddenly, over on the plaster in a brightly lit corner of the banquet hall, fingers of a human hand began to write. The terrified king called for help. "I've got to know the meaning of those words."

History repeats itself. Belshazzar, surely a chip off the old block, brought in the latest crop of wise men. "You've got the wrong department, sir," they said. "We don't do walls." There was such a commotion that the queen came running, assessed the situation, and quickly advised, "Do what always worked for your father. Call Daniel."

Daniel was summoned and offered a royal wardrobe, a gold necklace, and a job promotion—to third man in Babylon—if he could translate those four little words. Most of us can endure poverty, but not many can survive an increase in affluence and power. Daniel did. "Keep your gifts," he said. "Give the rewards to someone else. Now if you'll excuse me a minute, I'll tell you what those words on the wall say."

Before doing so, however, Daniel took advantage of a captive audience. He preached Belshazzar an angry sermon. I think those profaned temple goblets set him off. Here's his three-point outline:

Point 1: Your dad thought he was pretty hot stuff until God cut him down.

Point 2: His example didn't teach you a thing about humility.

Point 3: So you purposely blaspheme the One who holds your life in his hands.

Daniel's interpretation of *Mene, Mene, Tekel, Parsin* is almost anticlimactic: Your days are numbered, because God has weighed you and you've come up short. It's time for your exit. Make way for the Medes and the Persians.

Despite his protest, Daniel then and there was given the promised rewards and promotion. But that very night enemy forces swept in and killed Belshazzar.

I don't know about you, but I have trouble offering incisive criticism of folks, especially when they have some degree of control over my life. But if we're talking gospel here, it must be done. We have to give the bad news of man's shortfall before the perfection God demands. Even if we don't have Daniel's phenomenal courage, however, we do have one advantage he didn't have. Our three-point sermon ends with wonderful good news. God, in his incomprehensible love, extended his grace to save us. How can we be afraid if we really understand this?

The Ultimate Test

Nebuchadnezzar's kingdom was, as Daniel had prophesied, divided. The Persian monarch Cyrus had already come to power, and with the murder of Belshazzar, Darius the Mede took control of his part of the empire. In this historical context Daniel was about to undergo the greatest possible test in his commitment to God.

Darius appointed 120 provincial governors overseen by three administrators. Darius must have seen Daniel's good qualities; Daniel was appointed as one of those regional administrators. He performed his job well, rooting out corruption and inefficiency. Darius noticed and announced that Daniel would be his new, number-one man. Daniel was near eighty now, at the peak of his long career of public service. There was "no corruption in him, because he was trustworthy and neither corrupt nor negligent" (Dn 6:4). But there was a problem.

The other two administrators and their provincial governors tried to stop the appointment. Did they want younger blood? Did they object to his being a Jew? Was he too vigilant? Were they just miffed and envious? We don't know, but sensing how things work in Washington, we understand the scenario. When you don't want the appointee seated, you seek to disqualify the individual by attacking from every possible angle.

That's what they did with Daniel. They checked out his job skills. Outstanding. Corruption? Squeaky clean. Job performance? Still vigorous and sharp as a tack. Finally, some slippery character who knew something about Daniel's devotional life came up with the winning game plan: "The only way we'll get him is to attack his relationship with his God."

"But that's his strongest point!" someone may have objected.

"You think so? You just wait and see. We'll convince the king to make it illegal to pray to anyone or any god except the king—for just thirty days. Long enough for us to catch Daniel and do him in."

Perhaps you've been wondering how Daniel could have faithfully served the superpower that had destroyed Jerusalem and brought the people of Judah into Babylonian exile. Here we are finally able to peek into Daniel's living room and into his heart. His love for God was inextricably linked with his love for God's people—his people. Every day before he left for work, Daniel opened the shutters on an upstairs window. He knelt facing Jerusalem, 125 miles to the southwest, and he prayed. He went home on his lunch break and did the same thing. Once again, after work, the shutters squeaked open and Daniel bent his creaky knees to give thanks to God and pray for his people.

Give thanks? Whatever for? Thousands of God's people were in captivity, dispersed throughout the Babylonian empire. God's Holy City, Jerusalem, and his temple were totally destroyed.

Actually, there were many reasons for thanksgiving. (Three prayers a day hardly seems adequate.) But there were two principal reasons. Almost seventy years earlier, the prophet Jeremiah had risked his life to tell Judah to surrender to Nebuchadnezzar. He had known this tragedy was God's plan to bring his people back to himself. And now it was actually happening in one of the greatest turnarounds in the history of religion. The *International Bible Encyclopedia* (Electronic Database) notes: "Being without a country, without a ritual system, without any material basis for their life as a people, [the Jews in captivity] learned as never before to prize those spiritual possessions which had come down to them from the past."

There was at least one other overwhelming reason to give thanks. That was the promise of restoration. After seventy years in captivity, Jeremiah had said, God's people would return to Judah. Jerusalem, its walls, and the temple would be rebuilt

(Jer 25:12; 29:10). Daniel's fellow prophet Ezekiel, there with the exiles in Babylon, was joyously encouraging them to look forward to the day they would return to Jerusalem. Every day Daniel could pray, "Thank you, Lord, we're another day closer to going home."

As Daniel's enemies plotted to catch him in the act of praying, waiting for him to open the windows of his prayer room, Jeremiah's seventy years were almost at an end. God was preparing Cyrus to overthrow Babylon. The exiles would be released and a remnant would return to Jerusalem.

Is it worth it, Daniel, to risk your life so late in the game? Your long career is almost over. The captivity is about to end, and you know the king has published this edict. If you open those windows and let them see you praying, you're a dead man. Meat for the lions.

Daniel opened the shutters. As he knelt, he saw a group of men in the street below scurrying away toward the palace.

The commitment level of this great Builder is 100 percent. Threatened with a gruesome death, he would not for a moment consider ending his loyalty to God or his people.

I hear the thud of a body hitting hard-packed earth and I wince. Darius, very much against his will, has just ordered his soldiers to drop a faithful, eighty-year-old man into the lions' cage. His execution will not be tidy, but at least it will be swift and sure.

I think you know the rest of the story. The king couldn't eat his supper, spent a sleepless night, and hurried to the lion pit bright and early the next morning. The night before he'd wished Daniel well ("May your God, whom you continually serve, rescue you!" [Dn 6:16], and, sure enough, God had answered. He had honored Daniel's unshakable trust and sent an angel to muzzle the lions.

Few of us have had to put our faith on the line in a life-or-death situation as Daniel did. But many of us have jeopardized our reputations or careers by doing the right thing and then having to suffer for it. When this happens, we must learn to trust God as Daniel did. There are no guarantees. God doesn't always send an angel. And yet we trust. Even if deliverance does not come, we have satisfaction in knowing that God has been glorified because he was able to make himself known to others.

The king was impressed with Daniel's commitment and with Daniel's God. Darius issued a new decree, reflecting the impact of Daniel's relationship with God. It required that "in every part of my kingdom people must fear and reverence the God of Daniel" (v. 26). The king gives several reasons for his edict: God is living; he is eternal; he is supreme; he is a miracle-working savior.

I don't know what change the edict brought to the empire. Usually conversion by fiat is not too effective. But it seems clear that, as for Daniel, he remained faithful until the very end. I believe this unwavering commitment had an impact on Cyrus' heart, causing him to open the way for the exiles to return to their homeland.

Daniel lived to see it. He died the year reconstruction began on the temple. Did he know he would be a key factor in ending the captivity? Probably not. God doesn't want us to be faithful just because it will result in some history-making event.

But then again, you never know.

The Second Mile

1. Do you know of a college student who actually grew spiritually during studies at a secular university? How or why could this be the case?

2. Nebuchadnezzar renamed Daniel Belteshazzar (which means "O Bel, protect the hostage of the king"). How would you respond if someone, contrary to your wishes, gave you a name that conflicted with your belief in God?

3. Consider Daniel's special gift of interpreting dreams. Do you feel proud and egotistical, or are you humbled when God chooses you for a special task? (Or, if you're like Shadrach or Meshach and have a friend with a special gift not given to you, how do you respond?)

4. Have you been able to keep your balance and maintain your commitment to God, in the face of whatever honor, wealth, or power have come your way? How did a raise, a job promotion, or some special recognition affect your spiritual life?

5. What would your enemies say about you if they scrutinized your spiritual life?

6. On what basis do you decide to conform or not conform to people or situations around you?

7. What would you do if you learned that Bible reading or prayer was a crime tied to a stiff jail penalty?

8. Compare and contrast Nebuchadnezzar's and Darius' perceptions of God.

9. Can you think of a time of extreme pressure or temptation when you, like Daniel, were able to remain true to God?

10. One hardly knows whether to weep with the prophet

Jeremiah as he predicts God's chastisement of his people or to laugh with Ezekiel as he foretells the rebuilding of Jerusalem, the temple, and the Jewish nation. If you had been Daniel, what would you have done?

11. Can you recall a time when, at some personal risk, you "opened your windows"?

so you thought Felix and Oscar were the original odd couple?

Mary and Martha: Two Singles
Who Valued Friendship

For Mary and Martha's story,
see Luke 10:38-42; John 11:1-44; 12:1-11.

One was an Epicurean; the other wolfed down choles-terol-laden, fast-food sandwiches. One threw his dirty laundry on the floor; the other picked it up. They were natty, fussbudget Felix Unger and his cigar-chomping housemate, the ultimate slob, Oscar Madison. The ABC sitcom, starring Tony Randall and Jack Klugman, kept millions laughing from 1970 to 1975. Twenty-five years later we still watch Oscar and Felix on cable and wonder if their show, like Felix's wine, isn't actually improving with age.

"Can two divorced men share an apartment without driving each other crazy?" the show asked. The answer, spelled out loud and clear in each episode, was "just barely." And for good reason. Felix and Oscar weren't just two single men. They were two men who were the ultimate incompatibles. Felix went for ballet; Oscar for baseball. Felix was obsessed with neatness; Oscar cultivated slovenliness. Felix was upbeat, optimistic; Oscar was morose and pessimistic. The conflicts that emerged from these and many other consummate differences still provide us with an unlimited source of enduring humor.

In real life it's a little different. Personality conflicts are not funny. A marriage breaks up because he and she can't get along. At work there are certain people you just can't stand, but they're part of your department; you have to work with them. Or maybe it's the boss who drives you crazy. You tolerate him or her or find a new job.

Then there are friends and acquaintances. We need them. We want them in our lives. You need someone to move in and help pay the rent. Your car breaks down, and you don't have the money or know-how to fix it, but your buddy is a sometimes mechanic. You've got to move, and you just happen to have a friend with a pickup. God designed us to live in relationships, but sometimes we're so *even* and they're so *odd!* Why are they unreasonable, demanding, insensitive, unpleasant, while we are logical, giving, considerate, and fun to be with?

Marriage, work, and friendships are all relationships we have made some choices about. Families are different. We don't choose our parents, and we don't pick our siblings. But at least for a while we all have to get along well enough to live under the same roof.

Meaningful relationships are difficult to initiate and even harder to maintain. In this chapter we'll see this as we look at the original odd couple—and I don't mean Jack Lemmon and Walter Matthau on Broadway. We'll be watching three timeless episodes in the lives of two single women. Their names are

Mary and Martha, and they are so different, we'll sometimes wonder how they can stand each other.

Just like on cable, we're going to watch several episodes back to back. We'll be looking for principles that can help us through difficult times with people we're supposed to like. So let's say good-bye to Felix and Oscar. Why don't you flip the remote over to channel 10 (Luke 10:38-42)? We'll get started.

Sister Act

The setting for this first episode is in the home of Mary and Martha. The two sisters live in a little village called Bethany just outside Jerusalem. He's not mentioned here, but they have a brother living with them, named Lazarus. This three-some seems a little unconventional, but perhaps it's a matter of convenience. Is Martha a widow with a big house who has agreed to care for her younger brother and sister? Are the three orphaned, with Martha looking after her siblings? We don't know.

We don't know much about Lazarus either, except that he was much loved and will become the focus of a major crisis in the next episode. What we do know is that we have two very dissimilar women living together and trying to get along.

The action for this episode begins when a family friend, accompanied by twelve of his friends, drops in. The friend is Jesus. It appears that he and his disciples often stay here when visiting Jerusalem. So with the arrival of their much loved and distinguished guests, Mary and Martha scurry out to the kitchen to prepare the best company meal they can put on the table. "Let's see," Martha says. "Jesus and the twelve, that's thirteen, and the three of us, that's sixteen. You set the table, please, Mary. I'll get more wood for the stove."

The two sisters are off to a great start, but fixing a meal for this crowd is no small task. Domino's Pizza is not just a phone call away and KFC is not just around the corner. There are no boxes or cans to open, dump, and stir. There's nothing in the freezer, and if the menu is to include meat, someone will have to kill and clean it before it can be cooked.

Anticipating a delay of a few hours, Jesus finds a chair and his disciples find places around him on the floor. They're weary from the events of the day, but there's so much to talk about! "Lord, you look as if you're still excited about the debriefings with the seventy evangelists," one of the disciples comments.

Mary enters the room with a stack of plates and begins quietly setting the table.

Another disciple says, "I'm just amazed at the way you dealt with that lawyer today. He was so sure he could trip you up!"

At the dining table, Mary looks up and pauses, holding in midair a plate she's about to set down.

Another disciple speaks, "And what about that parable, guys? Did you ever think you'd hear a story about a *good* Samaritan?" The men all laugh.

Mary is fascinated by their chatter. She just has to be a part of this conversation, at least as a listener. She sets down her plates and rushes across the room to where Jesus is sitting. "Master," she says, finding a place at his feet, "tell me the parable. The one about the good Samaritan."

Jesus and the disciples hardly get started retelling the story of the priest and the Levite and the Samaritan, when Martha enters the room. She sees the half-set table and spies Mary, enraptured, sitting at Jesus' feet. She pushes a wisp of hair back from her moist forehead and looks at Jesus, her eyes flashing. "Lord, don't you care that my sister has left me to do the work by myself? Tell her to help me!" (v. 40).

A reasonable request? Certainly, but, to say the least, Martha's attitude is about 180 degrees out of sync. She chastises her sister for not helping with dinner, and she accuses Jesus of not caring that Mary is holding up the program—her program. And she spouts all this off in front of company!

Come on, Martha. Jesus doesn't care? Well, yes, you're right. He doesn't care. The last thing this man cares about is when he's going to eat or where he's going to sleep. Won't you be surprised, Martha, when he leaves your home early some morning without waiting for breakfast? (See Mk 11:11-13.)

Has the Lord ever gotten after you about straightening up your priorities? He did Martha. Notice the sharp contrast in the tone of Jesus' response. "'Martha, Martha,' the Lord answered, 'you are worried and upset about many things, but only one thing is needed. Mary has chosen what is better, and it will not be taken away from her'" (Lk 10:41-42). In other words, "Take it easy, Martha. Dinner can wait."

That's the end of our first episode with our dramatic duo. It's time for a commercial break. After you hit the "mute" button, I'll tell you what I think happened next in that tension-filled home in Bethany.

I suspect the room grew very quiet as each person sorted through his or her emotions. The disciples were thinking, *Martha deserved that, and more!* But they were hungry, and they wanted dinner. Mary looked on in amazement. *I chose the one thing that was needed? What was that?* Martha retreated into the kitchen in confusion. I think she knew she'd made a colossal social blunder, but she couldn't understand why Jesus didn't care that dinner wouldn't be on time.

We need to talk about that some more, so why don't you just turn the TV off until it's time for the next episode. The best way to understand why Martha has her priorities all mixed up is to contrast the personalities of Mary and Martha. You can probably see some of the qualities already. Others will be obvious as we continue. Look at these differences:

Martha	*Mary*
Leader	Follower
Giver	Receiver
Active	Passive
Task-oriented	People-oriented
Practical	Passionate
Talker	Listener
Compulsive	Impulsive
Traditional	Innovative

Do these two columns describe you and someone you're close to? Are the two of you compatible or incompatible? As irritating as these differences can be, they can also bring great benefits. Differences in other people often make us aware of weaknesses in ourselves. We don't like that, of course, because we'd just as soon not change. But if we're committed to spiritual growth, rubbing up against the rough edges of a relationship can be a positive and powerful motivator to bring balance and growth. In fact, many times I've found that it's the "odd" people in my life who most enrich it.

I think Mary and Martha were discovering this, learning to use their differences to help them grow personally and in their relationship rather than allowing the differences to make them resentful. They sure were given opportunities. For example, in this first episode, Mary and Martha both showed their love for Jesus, but in completely different ways. Martha was loving Jesus by serving. Mary, on the other hand, showed her love in adoration; there was no place where she felt more fulfilled than at Jesus' feet. These differences in temperament open a great teaching opportunity for Jesus and a great learning opportunity for the two women. Is serving bad and worshiping good? No, that's not what Jesus said. He told Martha that her sister, at least for this moment, had chosen the better of the two. "Martha, you're so busy! Here's a chance to learn something from your sister," Jesus might have said. And knowing that he faced crucifixion only a few months down the road, he might have added, "I won't be able to spend time with you much longer, Martha. Why don't you just sit down here so I can enjoy you both for a little bit?" Did Martha learn? She still had some rough edges, but the two women could relate much better the next time we see them.

A Grave Issue

It's time for the next episode of the Original Odd Couple, so let's tune in. This time it's an hour-long special that promises some intense emotion. The synopsis for viewers reads: "Jesus is unexpectedly detained, but manages to intervene in the death of Lazarus, a close friend."

Let's set the stage for this familiar story, found in John 11. Several months have passed since Jesus' last visit to Bethany. He's been teaching east of the Jordan River in a district called Perea. Mary and Martha's brother, Lazarus, becomes ill and dies. All the action centers on this crisis event. We want to focus on Mary and Martha's behavior in this highly stressful situation.

In this circumstance, the two women do not let their differences bother them. Instead, they are drawn together. They both send word to Jesus. "Lord, the one you love is sick" (v. 3). Jesus' response suggests that he was no more inconvenienced by Lazarus' desperate condition than he was some time back by the prospect of a late dinner. "This sickness will not end in death. No, it is for God's glory so that God's Son may be glorified through it" (v. 4). He's so certain of this that he delays starting the two-day trip to Jericho and on to Bethany.

Finally, after two days, Jesus calls his disciples and says, "Let's go, fellows. We're on our way to Bethany." After hinting at what he knows to be true, Jesus bluntly tells the twelve that Lazarus is dead.

As Jesus reaches the outskirts of Bethany, Martha hears that he's approaching and slips away from her sister and the house full of mourners to meet him. Her encounter with Jesus on the dusty road to Bethany evokes one of the great declarations of faith found in the Bible. "'Lord,' Martha said to Jesus, 'if you had been here, my brother would not have died.'" Is she scolding Jesus again, this time for not coming in time? Perhaps, but she tempers her complaint by adding, "But I know that even now God will give you whatever you ask" (vv. 21-22). Then she reveals her great faith by declaring, "I believe that you are the Christ, the Son of God, who was to come into the world" (v. 27). (We'll discover a little later that she may have spoken more from her head than her heart.)

After Martha's touching encounter with Christ, she hurries back home to her sister with a message from Jesus. "'The Teacher is here,' she said, 'and is asking for you'" (v. 28). Mary is out the door in a split second. The mourners, thinking she's going to the tomb, follow.

Mary finds Jesus, still outside the village. Mary's opening words are identical to Martha's, but Mary is again on her knees, at his feet. "Lord, if you had been here, my brother would not have died" (v. 32).

Do I sense a different tone in the repetition of these words? G. Campbell Morgan wonders if maybe Mary isn't saying between sobs, "Lord, I wish it could have been possible for you to be here." The mourners trailing Mary are all crying. It's too much for Jesus. He weeps with them.

Neither woman has any idea what is happening, although they both think they do. And despite their professions of faith, they certainly can't conceive of what's about to happen. Once again Martha has tried to get Jesus organized, reorder his priorities. Mary, on the other hand, sorrowfully accepts what both women perceive to be Jesus' untimely arrival.

The scene moves now to Lazarus' tomb. The mourners gather around Jesus, Mary, and Martha. Jesus has known for days what he's going to do. He turns to the mourners. "Take away the stone," he commands (v. 39a).

Let's turn up the volume on our TV set. I just know Martha is going to have something to say, and I want to catch every word.

"But, Lord, by this time there is a bad odor, for he has been there four days" (v. 39b).

Have you ever counted the times you've said, "But, Lord...." We're all Marthas in crisis situations. We're so afraid God is going to do something foolish or unnecessary. We want to preserve his reputation, save him and ourselves (especially) from embarrassment. But, graciously, God does not allow our well-intentioned ignorance to keep him from carrying out his will.

We see this when Jesus answers Martha's "but, Lord": "Did I not tell you that if you believed, you would see the glory of God?" (v. 40). Clearly there is a price to pay for the absence of faith. Jesus does try to be accommodating in the face of this lack of trust.

But once they actually roll away the stone, Jesus prays and thanks the Father for hearing his prayer. He knows where his power comes from, but he wants the mourners to know too. Then he yells, "Lazarus, come out!" (v. 43).

Lazarus, wrapped in grave clothes, hobbles out of the tomb. Was God glorified, as Jesus promised? Yes, he was. Everyone there saw God's mighty life-giving power that could overcome even death. When you see Jesus demonstrate that he is the "resurrection and the life"—you can hardly help but believe, as many of the mourners did that day.

We can give the TV a rest until the final, upcoming episode of the Original Odd Couple. But while we wait, I can tell you that Jesus really did love this household of single adults in

Bethany. How much? His disciples knew he risked his life and theirs when he responded to Mary and Martha's call for help. Their home was less than two miles from Jerusalem, where religious authorities were determined to find and kill him. Does Jesus love you and this odd person he's somehow allowed into your life? It's a foolish question, isn't it? He didn't just risk his life for you; he gave it up! That kind of love is hard to misunderstand.

Now if you'll click the power button on your remote, we'll get back to our story.

Sweet Aroma

Here comes our last Mary and Martha episode. This time we're in for a drastic change in mood. We're going from the intense grief of a funeral (in John 11) to the excitement and fun of a party (John 12).

To give you a little background while the credits run: After raising Lazarus, Jesus kept a low profile.

Now, facing his final countdown as a man living on earth, Jesus retreats to whatever safety Bethany has to offer. Simon, a leper friend of Mary and Martha, is honoring Jesus with a party. You can see Jesus there on the left, reclining at the table with the party-goers.

Can you guess what Martha is doing? Dinner is ready, so she's busy putting food on the tables—and it's not even her house! But did anyone notice? She's not distracted this time. I think perhaps she's learned something.

Lazarus is there, living evidence of God's power. His life is in danger too, but he's there at the table with Jesus.

Where's Mary? Not surprisingly, she's kneeling at Jesus' feet. Good.

And what do I notice here? These two women seem to be allowing each other to love her Lord in the way most natural to her own individual temperament. They're learning that that's usually the best way.

But I have to say that I think Mary is a little out of character here. She's not a public person. She's a listener. And a homebody. She's not the extrovert party girl who likes to call attention to herself. But on this occasion, her love for Jesus is so intense that it pushes aside any inhibitions she might have for what she is about to do. Regardless of what people may think or say, she is about to do something very unusual, and, as it turns out, controversial. (I doubt if she fully understood the significance of her extravagant act of adoration until Jesus explained it to those who criticized her.)

Get the picture: Jesus, with the other diners at the table, is reclining. Mary is kneeling at his feet with a pint container of expensive perfumed oil in her hands. Where did she get it? Did she go out and buy it just for this party? Was it something special she was saving for her wedding night?

Gently, she begins pouring the oil over Jesus' feet. As it begins to drip on the floor, she takes her long hair and wipes away the excess. The sweet aroma permeates the room and everyone realizes what this woman is doing there at the head table. Martha, if you have something to say, now's the time to get your sister back on the right track.

Martha, the compulsive talker, is smiling. She has nothing

to say. I think maybe when Mary let her in on her plan, Martha said, "That's great, Sis. I could never do anything like that, but I think it's just perfect for you. Look for me. I'll be doing my thing serving tables."

"You don't mind the expense? It came to a whole year's wage!"

"Mind? Nothing's too good for the Master. Simon will have the servants wash Jesus' feet with water when he comes in. You wash them with perfume."

The fragrant dining hall is quiet until one of the disciples rises. It's Judas Iscariot, the disciples' treasurer. "Why wasn't this perfume sold and the money given to the poor?" (Jn 12:5). What a party pooper! This man isn't concerned about the poor. He's been dipping into the till, and he knows funds are getting low.

Once again, Jesus defends Mary. "Leave her alone" (v. 7). Can you hear the stern authority in his voice? Jesus gladly receives and enjoys Mary's extraordinary gift.

Friendship Principles

I don't know about you, but I sense growth and change in these two women. They both had good reasons to say, "I give up. I can't live with someone like you. I need my space." I'm glad for the principles they used to bring harmony in spite of their striking differences. Let's recap these three Gospel episodes and identify a few principles we can learn about friendship.

1. Be accepting. Show respect. Appreciate your friend's gifts. I sense that these two women gradually came to see that they were complementary, not incompatible. For some singles, differences in preferences and temperaments loom so large that they see the person in front of them as a singular irritation. In *The Divorce Recovery Handbook,* John Splinter notes: "We judge ourselves by our intentions; we judge others by their actions or their behaviors."

It's easy to define someone in terms of their offenses, rather than as a man or woman made in the image of God. Rather than as someone who may have had good intentions. In a book titled *Friendship,* published one hundred years ago, Hugh Black—speaking largely to men—noted, "We do not treat our friends with enough respect. We make the mistake of looking upon the common as if it were cheap in nature. We ought rather to treat our friend with a sort of sacred familiarity, as if we appreciated the precious gift his friendship is."

2. Find common ground. Mary and Martha found at least one thing that held them together until they managed to do a little growing. In a healthy way they shared a mutual friend who loved them both very much: Jesus Christ.

In her book *Treasured Friends,* Ann Hibbard tells the story of lonely Juanita who prayed for a friend. Then, Juanita says,

A woman I didn't know well asked me to be her prayer partner. We were so different. She was single … with a load of pain and insecurity. I was a homemaker with teenagers.

Despite these differences, we've met every week for an hour for the past five years….

I've seen my friend grow in confidence ... and God's taken my loneliness away.

Why not ask someone very different from you to be a prayer partner? Ann Hibbard suggests you agree to meet together to pray for a specified number of weeks. Then you can reevaluate with minimal awkwardness.

This is just one suggestion for grounding your relationships in Christ—focusing and standing on the Solid Rock.

3. Find shared outreach. Jesus' association with Mary and Martha was during a time of great personal stress. Their home was open. He could rest there. There was always something to eat on the back of the stove. There was peace and love there when all he had experienced all day was rejection. Because they were interested in giving and reaching out, Mary and Martha invited Jesus and his disciples to their home.

In *The Four Loves,* C.S. Lewis contrasts eros with friendship. He notes that "lovers are normally face to face; friends side by side, absorbed in some common interest." What "common task" can you initiate with a friend to focus your attention on ministry, outreach, or even a purely enjoyable hobby? The memory and result of the shared task can cement your bonds of friendship. *(Do you remember the day Jesus and his twelve knocked on the door right at dinnertime and how we had to scramble to get a meal on?)*

4. Be real. Our relationships don't always run smoothly, just as they didn't for Mary and Martha. It's tough when love, trust, or commitment are tested, but if you can be real, you've got a fighting chance. Neither Mary nor Martha was afraid to be honest about the way she felt. They probably didn't always do it in the right way, and neither will we. But when you can count on transparency and vulnerability, a relationship can build and mature. Gary Inrig, in his helpful book *Quality Friendship*, asks: "Do I take the risk of openness, or is there a carefully constructed wall around my life that no one can penetrate? Have I ever expressed verbally my love and appreciation for my friend and displayed that love by opening up my life to him?"

5. Be patient. Relationships take time. Don't give up on that difficult person too soon. Be willing to give much more than you receive in the beginning. Decide ahead of time how you will relate to a controlling person like Martha. How will you get appropriate responses from a passive person like Mary? Take the time to work at it, to find out. Study your friend as your relationship builds, and you can grow together.

Beginning, cultivating, and maintaining friendships is not easy. The difficulty only increases when we are the "even" and the other person is "odd." (Rest assured, the other person thinks you're the "odd" one.) It takes time—our most precious commodity—and it may take great effort. And I suggest it takes a good bit of laughter, allowing ourselves to laugh with our friends about the wonderful diversity that makes for, well, never a dull day in the house of Martha and Mary.

The Second Mile

1. Mary and Martha seem to show different levels of spiritual

maturity. Which is the weaker? Should we feel free to criticize her? Why?

2. Of the three principals in this story, which one most exemplifies your forte: Martha, who serves; Mary, who excels in expressing love and appreciation; Jesus, who was there for his friends at a time of crisis?

3. Discuss or think about a time when your good motives were misunderstood (as Martha misunderstood Mary's intentions when listening to Jesus in the first episode). How did this make you feel? How did you respond? How might you respond if this happens in the future?

4. Suppose you are a "Mary" and your best friend is a "Martha" (or choose the opposite scenario). Imagine a conversation in which you are both showing respect and being honest and real. If you are studying this lesson in a group, role-play the conversation with someone.

5. When it comes to making friends, do you take the first step or wait for the other person to make the first move? Why do you think this is so?

6. Do you see personality differences in friendships as a plus or a minus. Why?

7. Think of a particular friend (or two) who irritates you. List up to five positive qualities about this person. Or list up to five things this person does "better" than you do.

8. What would you have to do to make Jesus your best friend if he isn't already?

winning at work without losing with God

Lydia: A Working Woman Who Almost Had It All

For Lydia's story, see Acts 16:12-40.

When Beth lost her husband in a tragic auto accident, she was devastated. Their years together had been happy. He had steadily moved ahead in a well-paying profession, allowing her to be free not to work outside the home. Both had been active in their local church, and now this! Insurance money would keep her solvent for a while, but she knew eventually she would have to get a job. She was only thirty-five, but she wondered what skills she had to offer. Who would hire her? And Beth asked another big question: Could she be away from her two grade-school kids forty-plus hours a week and still be a good mom?

As grief gradually relaxed its crushing grip, Beth spent part of most days at the local public library. She was amazed at the number of books that offered help for single mothers who had to support themselves. There was everything—how to write a résumé; how to resolve family-work conflicts; how to write a business plan, raise capital, and start your own business.

The more Beth researched, the more she saw that entering the workforce would require difficult compromise and painful sacrifice. But she made a personal decision: For her one of those sacrifices could not be leaving her children to someone else's care. She read case histories of mothers who chose to work but could not face the guilt they felt of "abandoning" their home and children for the workplace.

Beth read other case histories of single mothers who solved the child-care dilemma. They started home businesses. This minimized the problems and expense of child care, transportation, and an office wardrobe. Beth had a computer and she was an expert typist, so why not a home-based secretarial service? She made a few calls and found hourly rates ranged from twenty to twenty-five dollars. She prayed about it, sensed God's leading, and had business cards printed. Her first jobs came from her husband's former business associates. It was touch and go for a few months, but, as word got around, she soon had all the work she could handle.

Occasionally Beth's clients asked for services that were outside her normal secretarial work. They needed fliers and other more elaborate printed pieces. Beth felt she had the talent to do this work. As it seemed to promise a substantial increase in income, she invested in the necessary software.

So far so good. But life started to get complicated. Beth hadn't counted on the steep learning curve that came with several complex graphic-design programs. To keep up, she began working evenings, sometimes even before her kids were in bed. She mastered the programs, but as her expertise grew as a graphic designer, her workload increased. She realized she wasn't making time for personal Bible study and prayer—a part of her day she really enjoyed. Then in one week she got bad news, from her mechanic and her dentist. She needed a new car and both girls needed braces. More good reasons for accepting more work.

One morning Beth's phone rang. It was her pastor. "Beth, it's been several weeks since I've seen you in church. Is everything OK?"

"Things are great, Pastor. It's incredible the way the Lord is blessing me with work! You wouldn't believe the overtime I'm putting in."

"On Sunday mornings?"

"I'm afraid so. I keep having to get that 'ox out of the ditch.'"

As her pastor lovingly probed, Beth suddenly burst into tears. She saw how she'd gradually allowed herself to be sucked into a materialistic rat race. She no longer had time for God and was even neglecting her girls in ways she never dreamed possible. She made a counseling appointment with her pastor and resolved to work out a plan that would reestablish her priorities and bring her life back into balance.

Looking at Lydia

In some ways Beth reminds me a lot of Lydia, a businesswoman the apostle Paul came to know and appreciate during his second missionary trip. Tradition tells us this resident of Philippi in Macedonia was a single working mother, like Beth.

We don't know her real name. Lydia is just a nickname that indicates her place of origin, just as we might call someone

"Tex" because he came from Dallas. Lydia was a region in Asia Minor (now Turkey). We know her best as a "seller of purple," or, as more recent translations have it, "a dealer in purple cloth" (Acts 16:14). It seems Lydia had employees and operated her import business out of a spacious home.

Today anyone can walk into JCPenney and for a modest price go home with a blouse or shirt or jacket chosen from a variety of colors we call lavender, pansy, orchid, plumb, lilac, indigo—or just plain purple. Not so in Lydia's day. The wool fabric Lydia sold to her upscale clientele was worth its weight in silver.

The purple dye that made Lydia's fabric so expensive came from the small gland of a Mediterranean sea snail. Bromine from sea water concentrated in the gland; when removed and crushed, the milky excretion turned purple on exposure to the air. *Nelson's Illustrated Bible Dictionary* says 250,000 mollusks were required to make one ounce of the dye. No wonder there are still piles of broken murex shells near the ancient Phoenician coastal cities of Tyre and Sidon. And no wonder only the rich and famous could afford Lydia's product.

There is one way, however, that Beth doesn't remind me of Lydia at all. Lydia somehow managed to keep a prosperous business from crowding out her spiritual sensitivity. In fact, we see the woman who moved 250 miles from her native home to Philippi actually growing in her quest to know God. What was Lydia's secret for keeping her priorities straight? Is there anything she can teach us that will help us in our struggle for spirituality in our very materialistic world?

Before we answer those questions, we need to go back to the strange circumstances that brought Paul and Lydia together. Paul decided it was time to visit the churches he had established on his first missionary venture. After he and his companions (Silas, Luke, and Timothy) visited and strengthened a number of churches, their progress was blocked. Should they go into Asia Minor? Should they proceed northward across the border into Bithynia? The Holy Spirit said no. There was only one direction left to go, and that was west to Troas on the coast.

While there, Paul had a dream. In his dream he saw a man from Macedonia begging for help. Paul and his party immediately sailed across the Aegean Sea to the port city of Neapolis. From there they trekked inland nine miles, climbing a 1,600-foot pass and then down across the plain to Philippi.

Now put yourself in Paul's Birkenstocks. You've just received what seems to be clear divine guidance. You've promptly obeyed. Wouldn't you think something wonderful was about to happen? Paul approached the desk clerk in the Philippi Inn. "I was wondering if you could direct me to the synagogue. We've never been here before, and we'd like to hold some special meetings."

"I'm sorry, sir. This is a *Roman* colony. Philippi doesn't have a synagogue."

I don't think a frustrated Paul and company just sat around the lobby, but days passed and nothing significant happened. Finally Saturday, the Jewish day of worship, came. The Gangites River flowed about a mile outside the city gates. Someone proposed they go see if any Jews were there for ceremonial cleansing and worship.

I'd like to know whose idea it was to try the river, for, as it turned out, that suggestion would be critically important.

There on a little sandy beach, perhaps with some rocks for benches, the men found several women gathered for prayer. Paul and his friends sat down and began to talk with them. One of the women was Lydia.

It may have been obvious to Paul that Lydia, this transplanted Asian whom Luke calls "a "worshiper of God" (Acts 16:14), was a prime candidate for the gospel. The Greek expression used here to describe Lydia peppers the New Testament. It describes a non-Jew who sees Jehovah as the true God and "adores" him or "holds him in awe."

In Lydia's case it meant that she had thought long and hard about the gods of her girlhood in Thyatira. She surely had been to the temple of the Lydian sun-god, Tyrimnos. She had held in her hand coins stamped with his warriorlike image holding a double-headed battle ax. She knew about Boreatene, his female consort, and she had seen the temple dedicated to Sambethe where the prophetess lived. Somehow, especially after she settled in Philippi, these Asian gods didn't seem to make sense.

In her new European home, named four hundred years earlier after Philip II, father of Alexander the Great, Lydia found a whole new set of deities to sort through. She marveled at the temple to Sylvanus, one of the Roman woodland sprites. There were Roman gods and goddesses representing almost every facet of life. And as if that weren't enough, under this veneer of foreign culture was the original Greek pantheon. In *The Story of Civilization,* Will Durant notes: "There was something cold and impersonal in the gods of the [Roman] state religion; they could be bribed by offerings or sacrifices, but they could seldom provide comfort or individual inspiration;

by contrast the gods of Greece seemed intimately human, full of adventure, humor, and poetry. The Roman populace welcomed them...." What god should Lydia choose? Roman, Greek, or Asian?

There is still another important factor that could have either helped or hindered Lydia in her spiritual quest. In her day it was virtually impossible to engage in a given craft without belonging to a trade guild. These guilds, especially strong in Thyatira, Lydia's hometown, were very powerful. They were also closely associated with local pagan religions. Guild members went to feasts where they participated in immoral practices.

How did Lydia relate to her guild? Was she repulsed by the parties she was expected to attend? Did she eventually take a stand, leave her guild, and take whatever economic consequences they dished out? (Many in the early church did.)

We don't know how or why or when, but Lydia found her way through this labyrinth of the false to the one true God, the God of the Jewish people. He was not a god of nature, but the Creator. He was faithful instead of fickle, powerful instead of weak, pure instead of licentious. He inhabited eternity and was unchangeable. Her response as a Gentile was to worship this God the best way she knew how. She joined other like-minded women who met at a riverside prayer-place.

Lydia's Response to Paul's Good News

The point Lydia had reached in her spiritual pilgrimage was not unusual in the first century. Others who reached a similar milestone include an Ethiopian headed back to North Africa after a visit to Jerusalem. Philip talked with him as they bounced along in his chariot (Acts 8). Another was a Roman centurion named Cornelius. Peter went to the home of this "devout" and "God-fearing" man (Acts 10). Paul preached to Gentile worshipers of God in the synagogue at Pisidian Antioch (Acts 13). All these, like Lydia, were on the right track, but they had not gone far enough. What was lacking? What would you say to a person like this?

For any "worshiper of God," the missing element was this: knowledge of the good news about Jesus. Their knowledge of God was incomplete. I imagine Paul's words to Lydia must have been echoes of what he and Stephen and Peter had said previously: Jesus—Son of God and Son of Man—was crucified, but God raised his Son from the dead. He's the way to the Father. By simple faith in the Christ, our sins are forgiven. This makes everything right between you and the God you worship.

This was wonderful news indeed for Lydia. Her business had brought security and ample financial rewards. But somehow "the worries of this life, the deceitfulness of wealth and the desires for other things" did not "come in and choke" her spiritual desire (Mk 4:19). She was ready. Acts 16:14 says, "The Lord opened her heart to respond to Paul's message."

I wonder if Lydia was surprised at the way her life changed when she came to know Jesus. She shared her discovery with her household. They believed and with Lydia returned to the place of prayer at the river for a baptismal service.

When Lydia found Christ she sensed that a faith that fails to express itself in action isn't worth much. She immediately offered hospitality to Paul and his three companions, the itinerant missionaries who had shown her the way to the Savior. Paul was often reluctant to accept help from people where he ministered, so Lydia had to work at it. "She persuaded us," Luke admitted (Acts 16:15).

Before Paul and Silas left Philippi, they landed in prison and were released as a result of a violent earthquake. This in itself is an interesting story, found in the remainder of Acts 16. The story ends with another reference to Lydia: "After Paul and Silas came out of the prison, they went to Lydia's house, where they met with the brothers and encouraged them. Then they left" (v. 40).

For this unstoppable woman who wouldn't take no for an answer, hospitality was only the beginning. There is good reason to believe that the church Paul established during his visit met in her commodious home. We can even identify some of the people who attended. There was the local jailer and his family, whom Paul and Silas led to Christ. Epaphroditus was another; he later carried funds from Philippi to Paul during his Roman imprisonment, stayed to serve him, and nearly lost his life during a severe illness (see Phil 2:25-27). Clement was also part of the new Philippian church; his work with Paul received special commendation (see Phil 4:3).

In time, there were problem people in the church too. Paul later chided Euodia and Syntyche for their intransigence (see Phil 4:2).

Perhaps the slave girl, whose liberation sent Paul and Silas to jail, joined this growing group at Lydia's house (Acts 16). In his letter to the Philippian church, written during his Roman imprisonment, Paul also referred to unnamed overseers and deacons and an unidentified "yoke-fellow."

In addition to all that Lydia did for Paul and the local believers, there is evidence that her prosperous business allowed her to be a major financial contributor. Paul mentioned having received gifts from the church at Philippi. Although Paul is greeting the "saints" at Philippi, perhaps he had Lydia, his first convert, especially in mind when he wrote, "In all my prayers for all of you, I always pray with joy because of your partnership in the gospel *from the first day until now*" (Phil 1:4-5, emphasis mine). It is clear that the partnership included financial gifts. "Moreover, as you Philippians know, in the early days of your acquaintance with the gospel, when I set out from Macedonia, not one church shared with me in the matter of giving and receiving, except you only" (Phil 4:15).

Perhaps much later Paul was also thinking of Lydia and her contributions to the gospel when he wrote, "No widow may be put on the list of widows unless she is over sixty, has been faithful to her husband, and is well known for her good deeds, such as bringing up children, showing hospitality, washing the feet of the saints, helping those in trouble and devoting herself to all kinds of good deeds" (1 Tm 5:9-10).

In these and other passages it is implied that God used the gospel seed planted in Lydia's heart in a remarkable way. Paul's first convert in Europe and the church at her house prayed for and financed the spread of the gospel. Without this help, Paul would have found his first and second visits to eight or ten European cities difficult, if not impossible.

You may not view yourself as a Lydia, but God is counting on you, too, to respond to the gospel planted in your heart.

Just accepting the truth is not enough. God is looking for action that will prove your love for him and bring blessing into the lives of others. Isn't there someone who looks up to you? Be sure your life and your words influence that person for God. Has God given you an income? Use some of it to speed the gospel to those who haven't yet heard. Do you know how to cook, or do you have a spare bedroom? Let it be known that your home is a place where guests are welcome. You, in your own unique way, can be personally involved in doing something for Christ.

Perhaps some of this active involvement is easier for us today than it was for first-century Lydia. She couldn't leave her business or household, but many of us can. Hundreds of sending agencies are seeking short-term missionaries. If you're a committed Christian, it's as simple as naming your skill and picking your country. Yes, if you're a student, you'll have to take the summer off and trust God to make up for what you would have earned working. If you have a job, you may need to take a leave of absence or quit. But it can be done. This summer my single friend Cyndee will be witnessing for Christ in Africa. Paula will be in Russia. Scores of singles were among the large group my wife and I joined one summer, teaching English as a second language in China. Seeing the responsiveness of Chinese students to the gospel, several came home, signed a year's teaching contract, and returned.

Principles From Lydia's Life

"Great model," you say. "I'm impressed. What else can I learn from this first-century working mother named Lydia?" Good question. As I suggested earlier, I think that we, like Lydia, need to bring the material and spiritual parts of our lives into balance. Here are some concrete ideas that may help you rearrange your priorities.

1. Lydia realized she had not yet arrived spiritually. Lydia found the prayer meeting down by the river satisfactory. But then, as Paul taught about Christ, she discovered there was more.

We are all at different points in our spiritual maturity. As our knowledge of God increases, so will our ability to bring a godly perspective to the spiritual and material aspects of our lives. Lydia seems to have moved in this direction rather quickly. For some of us, it may take more time. The secret is to steer clear of that "I've arrived" attitude that makes us stop expecting and seeking spiritual growth.

For me, the best way to get off my spiritual plateau and get moving is to relive what I call the "Isaiah 6 experience." In his vision, Isaiah the prophet gained an overwhelming new perception of God's glory and holiness. Because he saw God as he really is, Isaiah saw the ugly reality of his own sinfulness. God provided the necessary cleansing and commissioning, just as he will for us.

I could wish for such a vision. It would be a thrilling, life-changing event. Instead, like Lydia, I find myself involved in a process of learning to know God. The process involves taking time to go to my place of prayer. It means focusing on Jesus Christ in my own personal study of the Word and as I sit under the teaching of those who know God better than I.

2. She knew she must respond to the gospel in its totality.
When we discover, as Lydia did, the fullness of God's revelation in Jesus Christ, we must allow God-made changes in our behavior and thinking. This is not as easy as it sounds. In his book *The Root of the Righteous*, A.W. Tozer explains: "Many of us Christians have become extremely skillful in arranging our lives so as to admit the truth of Christianity without being embarrassed by its implications. We arrange things so that we can get on well enough without divine aid, while at the same time ostensibly seeking it."

Not Lydia. The implications of her faith in Christ were in no way embarrassing. If the gospel was good for her, it was good for her entire household. Did Paul's little band need a place to sleep? She had extra bedrooms. Did the newly formed church need a home with a big front room? She had that, too. Did Paul need financial help for his missionary trips? He could count on Lydia and the Philippian church.

We know the measure of Lydia's commitment. How long has it been since you've measured yours? Look at your calendar. How many weeks or months has it been since you've shared your faith? Look at your daily agenda and your checkbook register. The way you use your time and resources will be a clear indication of your willingness to respond not only to the gospel, but to all its implications for the way you live your life.

3. She accepted the reality of the spiritual and the material. All of us live with the conscious or unconscious tension that results from living in two worlds. Many people disastrously attempt to get through life as if the only reality were the material. The other extreme is to deny the material side of life and try to live only in the spiritual sphere. History has shown that that doesn't work very well either. Apparently Lydia found a good balance between work and worship. As Gien Karssen notes in *Her Name Is Woman (Book 1)*, Lydia "did not, like many business people, become totally engrossed in her work. In spite of her many obligations, she found time for things of greater importance." How do you do this?

Sometimes we follow in the footsteps of our desktop publisher friend, Beth. We ease into workaholism and squeeze out the spiritual so gradually we hardly notice. Oh, there's always an excuse. I hear people saying, "The job has to be done, and I'm willing to make the sacrifice," or, "I just can't get by on my normal forty-hour pay." Then there are all those other activities that pile up. We keep saying yes to everyone who comes around thinking singles have more free time than married people.

In one of her chapters in *The Busy Woman's Guide to a Balanced Life*, Elaine McEwan-Adkins lists sure signs of overwork. Here are a few of them:

Waking up in the middle of the night to add items to your to-do list.

Not having time to celebrate your own birthday.

Leaving your clean underwear in the dryer for a week.

Sound familiar? If so, you might ask yourself why. Looking back with the twenty-twenty hindsight God gives, I can see that my sixty-plus-hour work weeks were always for all the wrong reasons. I was trying to keep up with another workaholic to prove my self-worth. I was trying to escape facing a problem that seemed insoluble. I felt guilty because there was so much to do and no one else to do it. And for singles, the temptation is to fill every waking hour with activity to escape loneliness.

You can get out of the busyness trap and bring balance to your life. The solution? In a word: reschedule. "Each week, schedule recreation, worship, social events, housecleaning, personal care, and shopping," McEwan-Adkins counsels. "When someone at the office asks you to do something extra, consult your calendar. If you've penciled in housecleaning or shopping, you have another commitment and can legitimately decline without apology or embarrassment."

If you still find it difficult to say no, remember that Jesus, in his brief, action- and people-packed ministry, was not tyrannized by the urgent. We can set our agenda and plan our days, but, in the final analysis, God is the one who has the right to determine what actually happens during our day. Charles E. Hummell explains in *Freedom from Tyranny of the Urgent,* "At the outset of Mark's Gospel, we find the secret of Jesus' ministry. He was not given a divinely drawn blueprint or advance schedule. Day by day he prayerfully listened for the Father's instructions.... In that way Jesus was able to resist urgent—even legitimate, at times desperate—demands in order to do what was really important, the will of the Father."

4. She saw that "things" were no longer of supreme importance. We don't hear Lydia apologizing for her big house or the luxury goods she sold. She turned her home into a place of worship and used her income to help in the evangelization of Europe. We all need to move beyond our view of "things for things' sake" to "things for God's sake." In *The*

Pursuit of God, A.W. Tozer says this of Abraham: "He had everything, *but he possessed nothing.*" I think this was also true of Lydia. How about you?

5. She knew emphasizing the spiritual over the material required a conscious choice. That choice may have meant she could not belong to a godless organization such as the dyer's guild in either Thyatira or Philippi. Her business associates in a city famous for its dyed woolen fabrics may well have thought she was committing financial suicide. Did wholesalers boycott her? Did she lose half her business?

For first-century Christians, belief in Christ often meant hardship, sacrifice, even imprisonment and death. Even here and now in this relatively free country, we are called to make choices—some that may cause us to agonize through sleepless nights. We have to decide what the focus of our lives will be and which bank account we most want to fill, the spiritual or the material.

Jesus' familiar words can help us make that decision. "Do not store up for yourselves treasures on earth, where moth and rust destroy, and where thieves break in and steal. But store up for yourselves treasures in heaven, where moth and rust do not destroy, and where thieves do not break in and steal. For where your treasure is, there your heart will be also" (Mt 6:19-21).

6. She did what she could do. It appears that Lydia found she could do quite a bit, but she couldn't do everything. For example, her circumstances didn't allow her to go to the mission field. Instead, she stayed home and helped support missionaries. We must not do nothing because we can't do a great deal. We serve God in the ways we best can, considering our unique gifts and circumstances. We can't do it all, but if our faith is genuine, can we sit idly by and do nothing? Lydia couldn't.

How closely does your success in bringing into balance the spiritual and the material parts of your life parallel Lydia's? Is your quest for more of God an ongoing process? Does the level of your service for Christ correspond to the reality of your faith? Have you realized that all you have belongs to God, and all you can do is give it back to him? Lydia answered these questions with a resounding yes. You can too.

The Second Mile

1. What evidence do you recall that assures you that Lydia truly opened her heart to the gospel when Paul presented her with the Good News of Christ?

2. How does Lydia's conversion experience compare or contrast with yours?

3. What abuses do you see today that result from material acquisition being a higher priority than seeking a deep spiritual relationship with Christ?

4. Have you ever had to leave an organization or a job because of your Christian convictions? What were the circumstances?

5. Have you ever tried to get off a spiritual plateau and "go for growth"? Did it work? Why or why not?

6. Is there anything that hinders you from knowing Christ

better? What could you do to break through that hindrance? If necessary, ask a close friend for help.

7. In your view, what spiritual price have you paid for working more than forty hours a week?

8. Try this for a week: Begin each day by giving it to your Lord. As his servant, allow him to bring unexpected people and events into your life. Thank him for the way he is continuing the good work he has begun in you. (Read Philippians 1:6.)

9. Do you know someone like Lydia who has taken those first baby steps to find God through Jesus Christ? How could you help this person continue his or her quest?

finding purpose for every single day

Paul: A Man Who Made the Most of His Singleness

For Paul's story, see Acts 9:13-28 and any of his letters.

His enemies called him a troublemaker, a babbler, a defiler, insane, a murderer—or a god. His friends called him a dear brother. We who look back on him from the perspective of twenty centuries see him as a scholar, a sage, a seer, and a saint; a Christian statesman, an organizational genius, a visionary, a loving pastor, a great preacher, a profound theologian, a persuasive apologist, and a master builder of the church. We marvel at his keen intellect and profound mysticism. We ponder his ailing, scarred body and are astonished at his enormous capacity for hard work.

He may be attacked or defended, but millions read every day from his writings. He's the first-century giant we know as the apostle Paul.

It's hard to exaggerate the lasting, worldwide impact of this single life. The first great writer of Christian literature, Paul penned nearly half the books in the New Testament. In his extensive travels he carried the gospel to Asia Minor, Greece, Rome, and perhaps Spain. Everywhere this pioneer evangelist went, he left established churches. And when the explosive issue of differences between Jewish and non-Jewish Christians boiled over, he welded the opposing forces into a unity he called the body of Christ.

Fourteen hundred years later, Martin Luther made Paul's teaching from Romans—salvation by faith alone—the keystone of the Protestant Reformation. Even today the life and teachings of Paul continue to influence and impact our world. How do you explain the singular impact of this astonishing man? Was he a genius? Yes. Did he enlist the aid of capable helpers? Many. Was he a hard-driving "type A" personality? Probably. Was his success due to his multicultural, trilingual upbringing? Can we attribute success to his superb education? Did it grow out of his passionate zeal? Did it result from his becoming God's "chosen vessel"? (Note Acts 9:15-16.)

Certainly all of these factors contributed to the amazing accomplishments of this Roman citizen who came from a respectable Jewish family in Tarsus. But over and above these elements, I believe there is a lens that converges every element of Paul's life into a single illuminating point of light.

The concave side of this lens diminishes the images focused upon it. These are legitimate parts of Paul's life he needed to discard if he was to reach his goal. It's not that they were unimportant; it was that other things were more important. Paul's classic statement in this regard is in his letter to friends at Philippi: "But whatever was to my profit I now consider loss for the sake of Christ ... for whose sake I have lost all things. I consider them rubbish, that I may gain Christ and be found in him, not having a righteousness of my own that comes from the law, but that which is through faith in Christ" (Phil 3:7-9).

What were the things that were once "gain" to Paul? "Everything," he says. "Take your pick." Start with education. Paul had the very best. It began in Tarsus, where he had studied the Hebrew text of the Law as well as the Septuagint, the Greek translation of the Old Testament. By the age of twenty, Paul had completed advanced studies in Jerusalem under the master teacher Gamaliel.

After completing his schooling, Paul probably returned to his parents' home in Tarsus. It was time to learn his father's trade of tent making. Probably during this ten-year interval in Tarsus, Paul married. Although he made no mention of a wife in his writings, marriage is implied because he later joined the Sanhedrin. Marriage and parenthood were requirements for membership.

But certainly he was not married when he wrote: "I wish that all men were as I am. But each man has his own gift from God; one has this gift, another has that. Now to the unmarried and the widows I say: It is good for them to stay unmarried, as I am" (1 Cor 7:7-8). The unsolvable mystery is what happened to Paul's wife, if indeed he ever had one. One possibility is that she abandoned or divorced him when he chose to follow Christ. I sometimes wonder if Paul was thinking of his wife when he wrote, "If any brother has a wife who is not a believer and she is willing to live with him, he must not divorce her.... But if the unbeliever leaves, let him [or her] do so. A believing man or woman is not bound in such circumstances; God has called us to live in peace" (1 Cor 7:12, 15). Still another possibility is that Paul was a widower. Whatever the case, it seems that he either willingly or unwillingly "suffered the loss" of his family.

In becoming a Christian, Paul said good-bye to family tradition and a certain religious status. His father was a Pharisee; Paul became a Pharisee. The Jewish sect was characterized by rigid observance of the Law as interpreted by the scribes. Members of this political and religious party paid special attention to tithing and ritual purity—the "tradition of the elders." An elitist group, Pharisees looked down on people less zealous than they in keeping the Law.

As a rising young Pharisee, Paul could have become a member of the Sanhedrin at age thirty. This august, seventy-one-member body was a sort of Jewish supreme court. It included the high priest, tribal heads, scribes, Pharisees, Sadducees, and rabbis. These men were permitted by the Romans to decide religious questions. Peter and John, Stephen, Jesus, and, yes, Paul himself stood before this court to defend themselves. This was a powerful, prestigious position, which Paul was eventually willing to relinquish in his commitment to Christ.

As if all this were not enough, Paul was willing to give up life itself. His affirmations on the subject are so well known that many Christians can quote them from memory: "But whatever was to my profit I now consider loss for the sake of Christ," he wrote in Philippians 3:7. And near the end of his life, Paul looked toward Jerusalem and almost certain death; he told the weeping elders from Ephesus, "I consider my life worth nothing to me, if only I may finish the race and complete the task the Lord Jesus has given me—the task of testifying to the gospel of God's grace" (Acts 20:24).

How can we explain Paul's willingness to give up so many worthwhile things? The answer lies in a complete turnaround in his value system. He says he considered them "loss." The word *loss* is the same word used in Acts 27, where Paul evaluated the danger the crew and his fellow passengers faced as their ship was breaking up in a storm. There would be no loss of life, he said. There would be, however, great loss to ship and cargo. So Paul's word choice—what was gain, I counted as loss—indicates that the things Paul gave up he considered truly gone, dead, lost.

Referring to his life-or-death determination, Paul used a metaphor. Why was he willing to give up so much? Part of him died so another part could live. "I have been crucified with Christ and I no longer live, but Christ lives in me. The life I live in the body, I live by faith in the Son of God, who loved me and gave himself for me" (Gal 2:20).

What to Discard?

How did Paul sort through and decide what he should keep and what he should throw away?

Well, we don't know all the workings of Paul's mind, but here's the way I make such choices. As an image or metaphor, I think it works to explain what Paul himself did. Perhaps you can use it too. I imagine my life as a big box. I know I have only one box, and it can contain only so much. When it's full, it's full. This means I need thoughtfully to choose everything that goes in. Obviously, I don't always do this. And even if I did, in time spiritual maturity would change the values I give various components. At any rate, my box is soon full. Then I discover something else that absolutely must go in. There's no room. Something of lesser value must come out. That's because our lives are finite. We mortals live and work under the constraints of limited time and energy.

When Paul became a Christian, the solution for his full box was drastic: Dump the entire contents on a manure pile! Like scraps from the dinner table, throw it all to the dogs! The entire contents were worthless compared to the new all-consuming, life-filling content he wanted to crowd into his box after he saw that flash of light and heard that compelling voice on the road to Damascus.

I have a pastor friend who, like Paul, had one of these improbable, later-in-life conversions. His business generated a six-figure salary. He had the home and all the toys that go with this kind of income. When he concluded that the Bible was truly God speaking to mankind, he realized there was nothing more important than mastering the contents of this Book and sharing it with others. He had almost completed graduate studies for a Ph.D., but this pursuit became of no consequence to him. He sold his business, his home, and most of his possessions and invested the proceeds in a seminary education.

How could my friend do this? How could Paul do it? A superb education, a business, home, prestige, and even life itself—all this is *rubbish*? It had become of little importance for two reasons. All these things had either taken Paul in the wrong direction or had somehow blocked him from going the way God wanted him to go. Now that he had turned around, he saw clearly that the superior must replace the inferior.

Suppose you love to fly. You save and scrimp and finally manage to buy an old Piper cub. You shine it and polish it and enjoy flying it. Then one day a millionaire friend takes you for a ride in his Lear jet. The luxury. The maneuverability. The speed! You can hardly believe such a plane exists. "You like it?" your friend asks. "I don't need it anymore. You can have it." You'd be a fool not to accept, but there's one small difficulty. There's room for only one plane in your hangar. Will you have a problem deciding what to do with the old Piper you loved so much?

If you look in your box and find nothing to dump in the garbage, something is wrong. Something in there is worthless, and, like Paul, you can let it go without remorse if you're convinced you're making room for other things of exceedingly greater value.

Now we come again to our imaginary lens. We turn it over, and the convex side enlarges and sharpens the picture we have of Paul's life. It does this by bringing together four positive rays that help explain Paul's profound impact on his world and ours.

A Single Pursuit: To Know Jesus Christ

Once Paul saw Jesus and realized who he was, everything else took second place. His desire to know Christ and be like him became the driving preoccupation of his life. Paul expresses this singular focus often and in a variety of ways. "For I resolved to know nothing while I was with you except Jesus Christ and him crucified," he wrote in 1 Corinthians 2:2. In Philippians 3:10, he said, "I want to know Christ and the power of his resurrection and the fellowship of sharing in his sufferings, becoming like him in his death."

In *Knowing God*, J.I. Packer challenges us with a personal application of Paul's singular pursuit. "What were we made for?

To know God. What aim should we set ourselves in life? To know God. What is the 'eternal life' that Jesus gives? Knowledge of God…. What is the best thing in life, bringing more joy, delight, and contentment, than anything else? Knowledge of God."

There are degrees of knowing, as Paul suggests in this passage. On the most superficial level are the people whose names we know. For example, one of my friends in Brazil might ask, "You know Ziraldo, the author of those wonderful children's books?"

"Sure," I would reply. "I have most of his books and once was even in the same room with him."

We use the same phrase, *knowing someone,* when referring to relationships we have with people we see once in a while. We know their names. We greet them when we see them at church, but we don't know where they live, where they work, or the names of their dogs.

Paul is not interested in either of these levels when it comes to his relationship with Christ. He wants the intimacy of a shared life. He wants to be close enough to draw from his companion's strength. When his friend suffers, he wants to share that suffering. If his friend dies, he is willing to die with him or for him.

Imagine, if you can, this improbable experiment. You are having a little dinner party for a few friends. You invite Paul to come as your honored guest. When he arrives, you see that he's brought a companion. There are introductions all around, and Paul says, "I'd like you all to meet my closest friend, Jesus." How would your guests respond? How would you respond?

I suspect you'd hear a few disinterested "gladtameechas."

They've heard that name but have no desire to carry the relationship further. Others would ask a few questions, make an effort to remember the face, so they could greet this man if they ever saw him in church.

Others (you included, I hope) would talk with Jesus for a few minutes and be totally captivated. You would get his phone number and invite him to lunch the first chance you got. You might even inquire where he was living and make plans to move to that city. Anything to spend more time with this phenomenal man! "Yes, I'm moving so I can be with Jesus," you would tell your friends. "The better I know him, the more my life will be like his. The more I'm like him, the more effective my ministry will become and the more God is going to bless me."

Paul wanted resurrection power for the daunting task ahead. He wanted the learning experience of suffering, and he wanted an ultimate abandonment to God's will and purpose, even if it meant dying for Christ. (Tradition tells us a Roman executioner's sword took off his head.)

If your first priority in life were to establish an intimate relationship with Jesus Christ, what would others observe about you that would convince them this was happening? If there's no room in your life for this kind of relationship, what garbage do you need to dump to make it possible?

A Single Purpose: To Communicate Christ

One-note people like Paul are not always fun to be with. I wonder if people ever got tired of his preaching? A young man named Eutychus did. Acts 20:6-12 tells the story: He became so drowsy that he fell asleep and tumbled out of a third-story window. Paul quickly took care of the problem and then continued preaching until daylight. I suspect he quit then only because the ship he was taking to Assos was about to go off and leave him.

Was Paul compulsive about his preaching? He says he was. "Yet when I preach the gospel, I cannot boast, for I am compelled to preach. Woe to me if I do not preach the gospel!" (1 Cor 9:16). There was nothing irrational about this irresistible urge Paul felt to preach. He knew he had good news, and without it men and women were lost and going to hell. "I am obligated both to Greeks and non-Greeks, both to the wise and the foolish. That is why I am so eager to preach the gospel also to you who are at Rome," he wrote in Romans 1:14-15.

This eagerness led Paul to leave some important pastoral duties to others. "For Christ did not send me to baptize, but to preach the gospel—not with words of human wisdom, lest the cross of Christ be emptied of its power" (1 Cor 1:17).

Was Paul's preaching always "user friendly"? It seems not. He gave people what they needed, not what they wanted. Paul knew the Jews were looking for authenticating miracles, the Greeks for philosophy. His response: "We preach Christ crucified: a stumbling block to Jews and foolishness to Gentiles" (1 Cor 1:22-23).

You could put Paul in jail, you could beat him within an inch of his life, and you could threaten to kill him. Nothing shut this mouth that ached for the next opportunity to tell someone about Jesus Christ. Not even his own low opinion of his preaching ability could stop him, at least not in Corinth. "I came to you in weakness and fear, and with much trembling. My message and my preaching were not with wise and persuasive words, but with a demonstration of the Spirit's power, so that your faith might not rest on men's wisdom, but on God's power" (1 Cor 2:3-5).

Do you sense something of Paul's urgency to share Christ even though you feel you may not be very good at it? Do you know anyone who does share Paul's compulsion?

I had a Christian barber once. Like all barbers he had the opportunity to spend most of his day talking to people. Ray loved football, and he had an absolutely encyclopedic knowledge of players, teams, and statistics. I used to listen to him talking to another customer, and I would think: *I wish I knew the Bible the way Ray knows football. What would it be like to be able to share Christ every day to a captive audience, such as a barbershop audience?* Somehow Ray never got beyond talking about his hobby. Not Paul. If he could have stood still long enough, he would have been the greatest barber-evangelist the world has ever seen.

A Single Love: The Church of Jesus Christ

To Paul the church was not a building or an institution but a body, a living organism. That body was made up of individual people, and he loved every one of them. I've often marveled that a task-oriented intellect like Paul could have such deep love and concern for people. It's a rare combination, but, when you read Paul's letters, you know it's true. He closes his first letter to Corinth with these words: "My love to all of you in Christ

Jesus. Amen." Near the beginning of his second letter, he says, "For I wrote you out of great distress and anguish of heart and with many tears, not to grieve you but to let you know the depth of my love for you" (2 Cor 2:4). To the believers in Philippi, one of his favorite churches, he wrote: "God can testify how I long for all of you with the affection of Christ Jesus" (Phil 1:8).

If love is best expressed in action, Paul knew how to do that too. He "struggled" for the believers at Colosse and Laodicea. In 2 Corinthians 11 Paul's writing takes on a heavy, ironic tone as he defends his commitment to the church. He "boasts" about the many times he's been in jail, flogged, stoned, ship-wrecked, been cold, hungry and naked, and in danger of his life. How could this church have possibly doubted his love and his concern for its strength?

Are you willing to suffer for something you don't believe in? Hardly. Paul believed absolutely in the viability of the church and considered any pain it caused him as part of his fellowship with Christ's suffering: "Now I rejoice in what was suffered for you, and I fill up in my flesh what is still lacking in regard to Christ's afflictions, for the sake of his body, which is the church," he told the believers (Col 1:24).

I'm afraid Paul's commitment to the church is not very popular these days. We go for what we can get (if it's not too inconvenient), not for what we can give. So we ask questions like these: Do we like the music? Are people friendly? Does the preaching make us feel good? If we feel warmed and well fed, we stay. If not, we look for something more appealing down the street.

And we especially look for a new pew to warm if we

become aware of some problem, as when leadership's overwhelming bias toward married couples results in discrimination toward singles. Or divorce is viewed as the unpardonable sin. Or the music is too traditional or too contemporary. We don't like the church when it doesn't work as it should. Paul didn't like dysfunctional churches either; he *loved* them. He fought for them, he protected them as a father protects an ailing child, and he gave of himself to bring them back to complete health and vigor.

If Paul were here, I believe he would encourage us to ask a different set of questions when we try to evaluate a church: What ministries are lacking in this church? Is there a niche where my gifts can be used? How can I encourage the pastor? What can I do to build unity and maintain purity of doctrine? What are specific needs and problems about which I can pray? How can I strengthen this church's outreach?

A Single Satisfaction: Seeing Believers Grow

Paul wanted those who found Christ as their Savior to grow (see Eph 4:14-15), to become complete (see Col 4:17), to be strong (see Rom 1:11), and to hold firm (see 1 Cor 16:13). He felt a heavy weight of personal responsibility to see this happen and worked hard at it. "We proclaim him, admonishing and teaching everyone with all wisdom, so that we may present everyone perfect in Christ. To this end I labor, struggling with all his energy, which so powerfully works in me" (Col 1:28-29).

Despite Paul's best efforts, some believers just didn't seem to want to grow up. Paul's harshest letters went to the spiritual adolescents at Corinth. They were expressing their immaturity in disunity, disagreements, quarreling, and hero worship. "I am not writing this to shame you, but to warn you, as my dear children. Even though you have ten thousand guardians in Christ, you do not have many fathers, for in Christ Jesus I became your father through the gospel. Therefore I urge you to imitate me" (1 Cor 4:14-16). He chided the Galatians for their inconstancy. "You foolish Galatians! Who has bewitched you? Before your very eyes Jesus Christ was clearly portrayed as crucified" (Gal 3:1). Later he added, "You were running a good race. Who cut in on you and kept you from obeying the truth?" (Gal 5:7).

Years ago I was in a doctor's office waiting to get shots for overseas travel. It was late in the afternoon, and when the last patient left, the doctor came out and showed me to a consultation room. "Did you see that woman who just left with the little baby?"

"Yes, I did," I said. "I wondered why they were here. The baby didn't look sick."

"Oh, but you're not a doctor. When the mother comes in for the baby's next checkup, I'll have to give her some terrible news."

I wondered that the doctor was sharing this confidential information with me. I expect he trusted me, as a clergyman. And I realized later his heart was breaking; he had to talk to someone. "Something's wrong with the child?"

"Her baby will never grow up," he said. "At best, the child will reach the physical and mental development of a four-year-old."

I didn't know how to respond to this tragic revelation. *What if I were the father of that child?* kept running through my mind. My heart would be crushed when I learned that my child would never grow to normal adulthood.

Paul hardly knew how to respond when some of his babies refused to be weaned and move on to solid food. He didn't understand. If they saw Christ as he had seen him, surely everything would change. How Paul must have rejoiced when he got letters from believers who were maturing in their faith. This kind of maturing Christian was his joy and crown (see Phil 4:1).

I shared Paul's joy when a single wrote this to me a short while ago: "During the past three years more deep and healing changes have been taking place in my life than ever before. My prayer life seems to be becoming the center of my life and growth. Recently I even started keeping a notebook of my responses to Scripture passages I read in my devotions. I never thought I'd live to see the day!"

On the back of a closet door at our house there are some pencil marks. Beside each mark is the name of a grandchild and a date. Before they were born that same door had marks that got progressively higher showing the growth of our own children. How many times that door heard someone say, "Take off your shoes. Stand up straight!"

Of course spiritual growth is not as easy to measure. But there is a yardstick. It's Jesus Christ. How far have you grown in becoming like him this year? Paul knew it was a lifelong process that wouldn't end "until we all reach unity in the faith and in the knowledge of the Son of God and become mature, attaining to the whole measure of the fullness of Christ" (Eph 4:13).

Joni Eareckson Tada knows how tough this process of maturing can be, especially when God uses tragedy to speed things up. As a teenager she had a diving accident that left her a quadriplegic. In an article titled "Never-Ending Journey with God" in *Virtue* (March–April 1992), Joni recalls the emotional and spiritual jolt she endured in her months in a hospital, lying on a Stryker frame:

> At night, after everyone else had gone home I would pray, "God, if I can't die, show me how to live, please!"
>
> Things didn't change overnight. But that simple prayer ... changed my outlook. I realized "growing up" was just something I was going to have to learn how to do.... What didn't happen through a Bible college or summer camp was done in months of struggle in the hospital.

Wanted: Imitators

A number of times in his epistles Paul says, "Be imitators of me." Paul was not perfect. He was sometimes stubborn or angry, and he himself wrote of other problems. In short, he was quite aware that he had not arrived. But to the extent that Paul was "conformed to the likeness of his Son" (Rom 8:29), the apostle wanted believers to follow his example.

Have you arrived? None of us is ultimately "there."

Are you just spinning your wheels and getting nowhere in your spiritual life? Follow Paul's example! Here are some questions you might ask yourself that could start you off in the right direction:

If I "took out the garbage," what things in my life would I need to dump?

How would others know that the top priority of my life is knowing Christ?

How effective are my words and my behavior in communicating Christ?

If I were accused of loving the church, would there be enough evidence to convict me? Why or why not?

What is the most notable spurt of spiritual growth I've experienced this year?

Here's a bottom-line question: Do I want God to use me?

Of course you or I may never accomplish what Paul accomplished. But God isn't asking you to put Paul's single-minded life on the altar. He's after yours, and he wants the exclusive rights.

The Second Mile

1. Draw a line graph charting the spiritual highs, lows, and plateaus of your life.
2. At specific points on the line, write in the circumstances or choices you made that inhibited or brought spiritual growth.
3. What part did difficulties and suffering play in your spiritual growth?
4. Read one of Paul's letters and identify verses that speak of Paul's:
   a. overwhelming desire to know Christ.
   b. irresistible urge to communicate Christ.
   c. love for the body of Christ—the church.
   d. joy in seeing others grow in Christ.
5. What specific action could you take to make one of these characteristics more real in your life?

single summa cum laude

Jesus: The Ultimate Single

For Jesus' story, see the Gospel of John.

Stan, a body-building hunk in his forties, was beginning to think romance would never come his way again. That was all right with him. He had many friends and was busy and fulfilled with his job as a restaurant manager and his life as a single dad. Then, as his girls grew up and left home, a loneliness he hadn't felt for a long time crept into his heart. Enter Nita.

Stan learned her name the first night she came to his restaurant, because she had to wait for a table. She was alone, and they chatted briefly before he seated her. She was not a ravishing beauty, but she wasn't bad looking either. What most impressed him that night was her easygoing manner and natural femininity. Nita came back again the next week. There were few diners, and they had a chance to chat further. She told him she was a professional photographer. She had never married. They both went to the same large church, they discovered, and ... would Stan like to see some of her photos?

To make a long story short, Nita and Stan got serious,

completed premarital counseling sessions, and got married. I thought it was one of those matches made in the heavenly match factory. When they got back from their honeymoon, Nita invited us over to see their honeymoon slides, which were, well, spectacular. But on the way home I said to my wife, "There's a marriage in trouble."

She disagreed.

"A picture's worth a thousand words," I explained.

"That's true, Confucius, and that's all we did all evening, look at pictures."

"How many pictures did you see of Stan?"

"Not any, now that you mention it."

"Think about it: A professional photographer marries a hunk. She takes photos on her honeymoon of nothing but rocks and trees?"

My hunch was right. Six months later Nita's ex-husband (she had lied about her previous marriage) called Stan. He tried to be tactful but didn't succeed. "Nita's seeing another man," he blurted. After the expressions of disbelief subsided, he added, "That's her history. I guess I should've warned you."

The divorce was quick and clean. Stan gradually healed, but the loneliness he felt became even more intense than before. Somewhere out there, he thought, there must be that ideal woman just waiting for him to dismount from his white charger and sweep her into his loving arms. He tried again. The results were equally disastrous.

Is there no perfect woman out there for all the Stans who are still looking for an ideal mate? Is there no model for all the unprincipled Nitas to know and emulate? Fortunately for all of us, there is. But don't blink. Of all the billions upon billions of possibilities there's only One.

He Knew Who He Was

Perfection—absolute perfection—is difficult to imagine, let alone describe. Those who wrote about the One who was perfect struggled with the concept. One of their more successful techniques was to assign descriptive names—more than 250 of them—to characterize this Perfect Being. Though we labor to understand who he was, he fully grasped his own identity. In fact, he was able to answer *all* the major questions philosophers and scientists continue to agonize over after millennia of debate and doubt: Who am I? Where did I come from? Why am I here? Where am I going?

I might characterize the life and ministry of Jesus Christ as a continuous, frustrating struggle to convince his contemporaries of his true identity. He battled especially with religious traditionalists, but even his intimates struggled with accepting him and understanding his mission. His greatest successes were with people with the deepest needs: the poor, the sick, and those who keenly sensed their own spiritual bankruptcy.

The many metaphors he used to describe himself are pregnant with meaning. His disciple John particularly loved to record them: He quotes Jesus as saying he was "the way and the truth and the life" (Jn 14:6), bread for sustenance, a light for clarity and understanding, a shepherd for protection and care, a door for a way to the Father, and a vine for life and fruitfulness.

Jesus also described himself in more direct terms. He said he was a servant, gentle and humble, a witness, a life giver, and the Son of Man.

Over and over Jesus purposely avoided direct statements about his identity. He wanted men and women to come to their own conclusions from the things he said and did. Once he asked his disciples who people thought he was. None of the guesses they'd heard came close. When he asked the disciples their own opinion, Peter hit it right on the nose: "You are the Christ." Then Jesus warned them to keep the discovery to themselves (see Mk 8:27-30). On another occasion he even told the demons speaking through two men near Gadarenes to be quiet when they shouted, "What do you want with us, Son of God?" (Mt 8:29).

Many simple people did discover Jesus' true identity. The religious establishment was something else again. With few exceptions, the threatened leaders who heard his words and saw his miracles remained very much unconvinced. In fact, the more the leaders understood who he knew himself to be, the more hostile they became.

It's essential for you, too, to discover Jesus' identity. Once you know him as the Son of God, the options are clear. You can either ignore him or trust him to be your way to the Father.

At the same time, it's also essential that you discover your own identity if you are to live a balanced, fruitful life. Who are you? Neil Anderson, a former pastor and seminary professor, likes to ask that question. He usually doesn't like the answers he gets. In his devotional book *Daily in Christ*, he notes:

But we tend to identify ourselves and each other primarily by physical appearance (tall, short, stocky, slender) or what we do (plumber, carpenter, nurse, engineer, clerk). Furthermore, when asked to identify ourselves in relation to our faith, we usually talk about our doctrinal position ... our denominational preference ... or our role in the church....

But is who you are determined by what you do, or is what you do determined by who you are?

The single most important element in the discovery of your identity, Anderson would agree, is found in your relationship with God the Father through Jesus Christ. If God is your Father, then you are his child. That would make Christ your Brother. You certainly picked a nice family to belong to!

He Knew Where He Came From

The Christmas story, as told at the beginning of Matthew and Luke, tells the unique circumstances of Jesus' birth. By virtue of his mother, he was human. By virtue of his Father, he was divine. Even as a child—talking to temple leaders—he indicated he knew who his Father was: "Didn't you know I had to be in my Father's house?" he told his irritated mother (Lk 2:49).

Today, when we read of the miracles and wonders of his ministry as recorded in the Gospel accounts, Jesus' divinity seems obvious. It was not obvious to his contemporaries. Because it was such a difficult truth to grasp, Jesus constantly emphasized his relationship to the Father. "I know him because I am from him and he sent me" (Jn 7:29). A little later he told people why they were having such a hard time knowing where he came from: "You don't know me or my Father. If you knew me, you would know my Father also" (Jn 8:19).

Taking another tack, Jesus explained that there were, as it were, two worlds. "You are from below; I am from above. You are of this world; I am not of this world" (Jn 8:23).

It couldn't have been any plainer! Jesus knew where he came from. His closest followers finally understood, but for most people, it was as if a supermarket tabloid had just announced the arrival of an extraterrestrial. The majority heard the news and remained as skeptical and unconvinced as Jesus' most hostile audience, the Pharisees. I can only imagine his body language when he said to them on one occasion, "I know where I came from and where I am going. But you have no idea where I come from or where I am going" (Jn 8:14).

During his later Judean ministry, Jesus had another heated discussion with the Pharisees, this time about spiritual parentage. At first they claimed Abraham as their father. Then when Jesus challenged this obvious physical link, they switched to the spiritual. "We are not illegitimate," they countered, maliciously calling to mind the questionable circumstances of Jesus' birth. "The only Father we have is God himself" (Jn 8:41). It's hard to be tactful with people as blind as these men were. Jesus didn't even try. "You belong to your father, the devil, and you want to carry out your father's desire," he said (v. 44).

That's a startling indictment, especially when it's pinned on someone who claims to live a godly life. Why did Jesus say that? His judgment was based on behavior. If these men were Abraham's children, they would behave as Abraham did; if God were their Father, they would love his Son.

So who is your spiritual father? I know, you go to church and even read your Bible and pray sometimes. But is there anyone who would contest your assertion that God is your Father based on *other* things you do? Jesus told those fanatical Pharisees that the key evidence of their relationship with God would be that they loved God's Son. People who love him, Jesus later said to his disciples, show it by obeying his commandments (see Jn 14:15). This makes love an act, not merely a feeling.

One of those commandments refers to love for our fellow believers: "By this all men will know that you are my disciples, if you love one another" (Jn 13:35).

He Knew Why He Was Here

Identification With Our Humanity
As I've said, Jesus was fully God and fully human. Only another human could convince us that he fully understands what it's like to be human; only God could undo the mess Adam left behind.

Let's look at Jesus' humanity. The tiny cells that locked in his DNA multiplied and developed in the warmth and safety of a woman's womb. In due time his infant body pushed through his mother's birth canal, and he was born. He grew as children grow and became a young man. His body had a normal level of testosterone. His feet got dirty and his wind-blown hair had to be combed. The sweat ran down his back as he climbed Judean hills on a warm day. He felt the pulsing of his heartbeat, got tired and thirsty. He sat down to rest. He ate. He slept. He urinated. And he bled, as we do when sharp instruments invade our bodies.

These are the everyday superficialities of our humanity. Jesus experienced every one of them, but being human is much more than any or all of these. In his concise, hurry-up style, Mark gets us right into one of these crucial human experiences before he's halfway through the first chapter of his Gospel: "At once the Spirit sent him out into the desert, and he was in the desert forty days, being tempted by Satan" (Mk 1:12).

Temptation? Jesus was tempted? Yes, for how else could he "sympathize" with our tendency to make wrong choices if he himself had not been subjected to similar enticements? (see Heb 4:15).

A cursory reading of Matthew's fuller account of Christ's temptation in the desert will hardly convince us that Jesus was tempted in any, let alone every, way that we humans are tempted. The three choices the devil offered—turn stones to bread, jump into 362 feet of nothingness, and accept the kingdoms of the world—seem little connected to most of our lives today.

However, if you read between the lines, the "everyman" quality of Christ's temptations is evident. In the first test, Satan asked, "Do you have physical needs?" In the second, "Do you have faith?" Finally, he asked, "Do you want power?" The answer to all the questions was a legitimate yes. So where is the evil in these enticements? Actually the test was not about making bread, taking a suicidal leap, or gaining power. It was whether or not Christ would go beyond the limits established by the Father to gain what Satan offered. Does a hungry man deserve food? May we not demonstrate our trust in God? Can't we have now the power that will ultimately be ours? These are the kinds of temptations I face every day. So do you.

Philip Yancey, in his disarmingly honest quest for *The Jesus I Never Knew,* sees this "showdown in the desert" as the ultimate test of Christ's humanity. "*If you are God,* said Satan, *then dazzle me. Act like God should act.* Jesus replied, *Only God makes those decisions, therefore I do nothing at your command.*" Nothing that is human was alien to Jesus, except sin.

How many times this week have you been tempted to betray your humanity and play God? How frequently do you say, "This is a legitimate need of mine, and it's within my power to satisfy it, so I will"? And how often have you been eager to take a shortcut to grasp something wonderful God wanted to give you eventually, as he had in mind a process that involved painful training and difficult course corrections?

The problem with surrendering to temptation is that there's a price to be paid. The price for us, as it would have been for Christ, is to allow ourselves to be subject to Satan's domination. To gain immediate possession of those legitimate and pleasurable things that a God who seems strangely uncomprehending keeps from us, we become Satan's slaves. Jesus was the singular exception to this human penchant to sin. Though tempted, he never sinned by yielding to temptation. His perfection completely satisfied the Father's requirements for a redeemer.

Vocational Identification

Jesus taught a mind-boggling truth to a group of twelve intimates. Jesus explained that he, too, had a vocation. He, the
Lord of the universe, was on a level lower than, say, fishermen
and tax collectors. He took the job nobody else wanted. He
became a servant, their servant. His symbol was the towel he
used to wash the feet of his uncomprehending disciples during
his last week on earth (see Jn 13:5-10).

In our culture we might understand what the disciples felt if
we imagined this unlikely scenario: The president of General
Motors gives up his stretch limo and turns in the key to his
posh executive suite. He decides to explore the life of the
working man as a caddie, an office boy, an orderly dumping
bedpans, a dishwasher, a bellhop, or a lowly gofer.

I recall a customer who came into a shop where I once
worked. My boss knew she came from our county's wealthiest
neighborhood and took time to strike up a conversation while
I put the finishing touches on her order. "And what does your
husband do?" my employer asked.

Grossly offended, the woman stiffened and hissed between
clenched teeth, "Why *nothing,* of course!"

It was not offensive to Jesus when he took the job few
people wanted to fill. He came as a king but voluntarily laid
aside his purple robes and took up a servant's towel. He could
have come as a CEO, or a white- or blue-collar worker, but he
chose the lowest rung on the vocational scale: the servant.
Like any servant, his prime concern was to respond to the
needs of others, with little concern for himself.

I don't blame the disciples too much for not understanding.
I struggle with the idea myself. Is it really true? "For even the

Son of Man did not come to be served, but to serve, and to give his life as a ransom for many" (Mk 10:45). It must be true. Jesus himself spoke those words.

Later, after Jesus died and returned to the Father, the apostle Paul reworked the idea of divine servanthood in a memorable passage, Philippians 2:5-11. It speaks directly to us and to our need to learn what was so difficult for Jesus' status-obsessed disciples. (In Mark 10:35-41 James and John vied for positions of honor beside Jesus' kingdom throne.)

> Your attitude should be the same as that of Christ Jesus:
> Who, being in very nature God,
> did not consider equality with God something to be
>   grasped,
> but made himself nothing,
>   taking the very nature of a servant,
>   being made in human likeness.
> And being found in appearance as a man,
>   he humbled himself
>   and became obedient to death—
>   even death on a cross!
> Therefore God exalted him to the highest place
>   and gave him the name that is above every name,
>   that at the name of Jesus every knee should bow,
>   in heaven and on earth and under the earth,
> and every tongue confess that Jesus Christ is Lord,
>   to the glory of God the Father.

Emotional Identification

Christ also identified with us in our humanity in the realm of emotions he felt. He hurt emotionally (and physically), just as we do, although psychological pain was not the only emotion he experienced. Some of the most poignant scenes in the life of Christ are ones in which we are explicitly told about his feelings: his anger when driving the merchants and moneychangers from the temple; his astonishment when he found unexpected faith; his fear when a mob threatened to stone him; his compassion for a hungry crowd; his joy after the debriefing of his seventy missioners; his sorrow over an unrepentant Jerusalem; his grief over the death of a dear friend, Lazarus; his impatience when his disciples didn't understand repeated teaching; and his intense anguish as he anticipated his own death.

During his three-year ministry, Jesus reacted emotionally to the stress of constant rejection and misunderstanding. Then, his public ministry ended, he had to endure one final week so intensely touched by physical and emotional pain that we call it Passion Week. How human that the Son of God should reveal his most acute emotions in the face of physical suffering!

In a *Christianity Today* article titled "The Emotions of Jesus" (February 3, 1997), G. Walter Hansen gives incisive impressions of a God with intense human emotions: "not a twinge of pity, but heartbroken compassion; not a passing irritation, but a terrifying anger; not a silent tear, but groans of anguish; not a weak smile, but ecstatic celebration." He hurt for others, and he hurt for himself.

But does Jesus really understand pain as we know it here and now? Does he see my tears when my son or daughter says his or her marriage is breaking up? Does he know the acute distress felt in the face of failure and separation? Does he know the despair my wife and I felt as we walked away from the caskets of our only son and youngest daughter? Yes, he does. The Son of God fought for his last few lungfuls of air on the cross as his Father looked away. He understands the agony of alienation.

An illustration from the fourteenth century brings home the truth that our God, who is Love, knows our pain. In anguish, Catherine of Siena once cried, "My God and Lord, where were you when my life was plunged in darkness and filth?" She says she heard a voice saying, "My daughter, did you feel it? I was in your heart." Commenting on Catherine's experience, Dennis Ngien notes, "Because our Lord knows pain firsthand, we can pray with confidence that he will be moved by our cries" ("The God Who Suffers," *Christianity Today*, February 3, 1997).

In every way Jesus felt what we feel. He knew the constraints of time and energy. He knew about daily pressure, pressure so intense there was no time to eat and nights were too short for sleep. But isn't it curious: Christ suffered to become like one of *us;* we suffer to become more like *him.*

The Second Adam

Are you getting the idea that Christ really did know why he came? The best way God could reach humankind was to send a God-human who could share the experience of our humanity. Christ's second major purpose in coming was to undo the mess Adam left behind. This being a book about singles, we dropped Adam's storyline rather abruptly once Eve entered the picture. Adam's union with Eve may have been the only marriage really made in heaven, but this perfect couple soon experienced imperfection. They chose to rebel against their Creator and moved away from an Edenic eternity to mortality in a sin-blighted world.

It's hard to overestimate the awfulness of sin in the world. Its bitter fruit appeared almost immediately. Man found himself alienated from God, creation, his fellow man, and himself. This crippling breakdown of four relationships has resulted in incalculable suffering from the problems humanity seems much better at exacerbating than solving.

If only there could be a kind of *second* Adam, someone who could start over and set things right! Fortunately for us there is. Paul develops this fascinating concept in Romans 5 and 1 Corinthians 15. From these and other passages, we find almost limitless comparisons and contrasts of the two Adams. In summary, there were two men, two choices, and two results. Let's look in greater detail at some of the similarities of these two men.

The two Adams, the first and the second, as Paul calls them, were both special creative acts of God. Both were given life and experienced death. Adam was man created in God's image. Christ was God made in man's image. Both were perfect and both dialogued with the devil. Both were tempted to acknowledge Satan's supremacy. Although Adam was not deceived by Satan, he chose to give up his life for his bride, just as Christ gave his life for his bride, the church. God's Word was a crucial point of reference for both Adams' satanic encounters in which each man faced three avenues of temptation. The responses of both men brought unimaginable suffering. A final similarity: Both men became representative heads of the two divisions of the human race: the redeemed and the lost.

The contrasts between the two Adams from Genesis 3 and Romans 5 are perhaps even more striking.

First Adam	*Second Adam*
Natural	Spiritual
Plenty in a paradise	Desperate need in a desert
Man tempted to be God	God tempted not to be man
Use the tree	Avoid the tree
Satan seeks dominance of man	Satan seeks supremacy over God
Takes	Gives
Chooses personal gain	Resists personal gain
Disobedience	Obedience
Loses innocence	Keeps holiness
Many ruined	Many redeemed
Death	Life

The bottom line is that the Second Adam did succeed completely in cleaning up the tragic mess the first Adam left. The first sinless Adam was brought into an Edenic harmony where he had every chance to succeed. He chose personal gain and brought death to humankind. Christ, the Second Adam, came into this world's sinful chaos with every chance for failure. He resisted personal gain, remained loyal to his Father, and brought salvation to the world.

What does all this mean for you, a single living two thousand years later? It means that God, through Christ, has done everything he possibly can to show you he cares. He sent his Son to identify with you as a human. He experienced normal human reactions to the joys and sorrows of earth. God was even willing that his Son would experience the ultimate human suffering, an excruciatingly painful death.

Years ago my wife and I seriously considered becoming Brazilian citizens. As residents, we expected to spend our lives there. By changing our passports, we could enjoy all the rights of citizenship denied to us as aliens. On the other hand, we reasoned, if we became citizens of Brazil we would have to give up our United States citizenship and all its rights and privileges. Should we leave things as they were, or should we take the big leap? In the end we chose to retain our United States citizenship. We believed we would lose more than we gained by becoming citizens of Brazil.

You and everyone else face a similar choice. You need to choose which Adam will be your representative head. It's not an easy choice, for there are certain rights and privileges of living under the first Adam. He allows you to pretty much do what you want. You can exercise your God-given human freedom, making your own independent choices, just as he did. Certainly you alone best know the choices that will bring fulfillment and significance to your life. Go for it!

No, wait! Don't go for it. There's that other Adam, the second one. He begs you to leave the kingdom of the first Adam and become a citizen of his kingdom. He doesn't promise it will always be easy, but he does promise he will always be there at your side, sustaining, comforting, and keeping you until the new paradise he's preparing for you is ready.

He Knew Where He Was Going

During the later part of his ministry, Christ spoke increasingly of leaving this world and returning to his Father. "I came from the Father and entered the world; now I am leaving the world and going back to the Father" (Jn 16:28). He had completed the brief ministry God had entrusted to him, and now it was time to go back home.

Even with all the disagreeable things about life on this planet, it's difficult for us to adopt Jesus' pilgrim mentality, to trade the impermanent—the only thing we know—for the eternal. Yet I'm strongly encouraged to take this unnatural view when I remember how Jesus prayed for me just before he died. Open the Gospel of John and read this wonderful prayer: John 17:8-21, particularly verses 8-11, 15-16, 20-21.

I willingly chose to be under this Second Adam, and two thousand years before I made my decision, he prayed for me! He knew that I, too, was not intended to be of the first Adam's world, and he wanted—still wants—me and you to spend eternity with him and his Father.

I don't know about you, but I find it daunting to be with someone who knows all the answers. And here we are, face to face with the consummate single, someone who effortlessly answers the four foundational questions of our existence. Are we, too, obliged to answer these four questions?

The answer is yes if we are to be the whole, spiritually productive people God intended. In this broken world we must know who we are, where we came from, why we are here, and where we are going. And we must be careful about the source of our answers. If we depend on human intelligence and experience, our conclusions will always be uncertain, tentative, and usually wrong! The only certain answers come from the perspective of an omniscient God in his revelation to humankind.

I've found my answers to the first three questions in the beginning of Paul's prayer in Ephesians 1:3-8. Because I believe these words are as true for me as for the believers in Ephesus, I pray this prayer often, making it my own by substituting first-person pronouns. Go ahead, open your Bible, and read the prayer.

Who am I? I'm the adopted son through Jesus Christ (v. 5). You may be the King's daughter, but this identification through relationship far supersedes our sexuality. Once we belonged to another spiritual family and were satisfied to live under a completely different code of behavior (see Eph 2). Now this new relationship has changed everything.

Where did I come from? Paul only hints at the answer to this question when he reminds me that I was chosen "before the creation of the world" (v. 4). This takes us clear back to Genesis 1, where this book started. God made me! (Compare Psalm 139.) Why is it that when we look at a magnificent building, an automobile, or a computer, we automatically come to the conclusion: These things exist for a purpose, and they would not exist were it not for the intelligence and design that brought them into being? So can this incredibly complex, thinking, self-aware organism called human be the result of random chance? Or is humankind the supreme evidence of a Creator who, even before he brought into being the formless and empty earth, made provision for me to have a loving relationship with him? God was there. He knows what happened, and he has shared it with us. Surely we must interpret science's theories of the origin of humanity by the Bible and not the other way around.

Why am I here? If an intelligent God made me, he must have had a purpose. Paul says it is that I might be redeemed and live "to the praise of his glorious grace" (vv. 5-6). Every Christian must believe this, but it's easy to get lost if we try to explain what this might mean. For a long time I thought it meant sanctification, spiritual maturity, or becoming Christlike. It does, but what does all that mean? It means that we are capable of spiritual reproduction. We live for Christ so that others might want to become a part of his family. We tell people about the Savior because we want them to be blessed "with every spiritual blessing in Christ" (v. 3), just as we are.

Where am I going? Because of my identification with Christ, my destiny is inexorably fixed. I will spend eternity with my Redeemer. To paraphrase Paul's declaration in Philippians 1:21: To live is to enjoy some of Christ for a lifetime; to die is to enjoy all of him forever. It's one of those win-win situations so obvious that many people miss it. God's answers to these four questions change everything. Now this perfect single named Jesus is my Friend, my Brother, my Savior. I kneel in awe. I will joyfully live for him in the knowledge that it was he who made it possible for a loving heavenly Father to put his arms around me and say to one more profligate child, "Welcome home!"

The Second Mile

1. Does the idea of a perfect single make you nervous, or does it make you feel good? Why?

2. Henrietta Mears was a single woman who had a tremendous influence on Christian education and publishing in the 1940s and 1950s. In his book of biographical sketches of influential Christian American singles, titled *Movers and Shapers,* Harold Ivan Smith tells of someone asking Mears why she had never married. She said it was "because she had not lived in the same dispensation as the Apostle Paul. Moreover, she had never found anyone, in this age, to match him, although she kept looking." Discuss her humorous quip in terms of having (or not having) reasonable and realistic expectations of a potential spouse.

3. Why do you think Christ had such a difficult time convincing people who he really was? What barriers to belief still exist?

4. How do you answer these four questions: Who am I? Where did I come from? Why am I here? Where am I going? Rate yourself (on a scale of one to five) on the certainty of your answers.

5. Does the fact that Jesus experienced emotions just as we do make you feel closer to him? Why?

6. Looking back at the contrast between Adam and Christ, could you summarize the two columns in two words? Hint: Death and Life. Try for several other pairs.

7. Have you ever changed your spiritual citizenship? Share the circumstances with a friend.

8. Read 1 Corinthians 15:20-49 and complete your own con-

trasting analysis of the two Adams. Divide a sheet of paper into two vertical columns, titled "First Adam" and "Second Adam." The entry for verses 20-23 might be: Brought death. Brought life. (Hint: Skip verses 29-41, which deal with the resurrection.)

9. Based on your study of 1 Corinthians 15, make some generalized statements about the nature of God and humanity, good and evil, obedience and disobedience, the blessing and curse of human free will.

10. What objections do you think an unbeliever might raise if you explained the concept of the two Adams?